The Economics of Partition

A Historical Survey Of Ireland In Terms Of Political Economy

ATHOL BOOKS
10 Athol Street
Belfast
BT12 4GX

Also by Brendan Clifford

The Life And Poems Of Thomas Moore
The Veto Controversy (including Thomas Moore's "A Letter To The Roman Catholics Of Dublin, 1810)
The Dubliner: The Lives, Times & Writings Of James Clarence Mangan
Connolly: The Polish Aspect
Derry And The Boyne: A Contemporary Account Of The Siege Of Derry, The Battle Of The Boyne and the General Condition of Ireland in The Jacobite War by Nicholas Plunket (Introduction: Brendan Clifford)
The Origins Of Irish Catholic Nationalism (reprints from Walter Cox's **Irish Magazine**, 1807-1815)
Ireland In The Great War (The Irish Insurrection of 1916 Set In Its Context Of The World War by Charles James O'Donnell (1849-1934) and Brendan Clifford)

About The United Irishmen:
Thomas Russell And Belfast (a biography of "the man from God knows where", the Munster soldier who was central to the social life of Belfast in the United Irish phase, and was executed for his part in Emmet's Rebellion)
Scripture Politics: Selections From The Writings Of Rev. William Steel Dickson, The Most Influential United Irishman Of The North (edited By B. Clifford)
Billy Bluff And The Squire (A Satire On Irish Aristocracy) And Other Writings by Rev. James Porter, Who Was Hanged In The Course Of the Rebellion (ed. BC)
The Causes Of The Rebellion In Ireland and Other Writings by Rev. Thomas Ledlie Birch (Selected And Introduced by B. Clifford)
Belfast In The French Revolution

The Economics Of Partition
A Historical Survey Of Ireland In Terms Of Political Economy
by Brendan Clifford
ISBN 0 85034 056 X
First published by the British & Irish Communist Organisation, January 1969.
This book is a reprint of the Revised and Extended 4th Edition
published by the B&ICO, 1972.

Published by
Athol Books,
**10 Athol Street,
Belfast,
BT12 4GX.**

© **Athol Books 1992**

This book is sold subject to the condition that it shall not, by way of trade or otherwise, be lent, resold, hired out, or otherwise circulated without the publisher's prior consent in any form of binding or cover other than that in which it is published and without a similar condition including this condition being imposed on the subsequent purchaser.

Contents

	Page
Introduction	5
Preface To Revised And Extended 1972 (4th) Edition	9
Economics And Partition	11

Ulster Custom
{Origin; Clansmen And Tenants; Gavan Duffy; Montgomery; Ulster Protestant Views; The Ulster Scot; The Devon Commission; Development Of Tenant-Right; How Tenant-Right Was 'Allowed' In Ulster; Davis And The Aristocracy; The Political Economy Of Tenant-Right; The Imperialist View; Lecky's Lament.}   15

The Linen Trade
{The Development Of The Linen Industry; Who Was 'Favoured'?; The Sinn Fein View; *Appendix:* Cotton; Wool & Linen; Wool.}   36

Grattan's Parliament
{*Appendix:* Greaves; Trotskyists; Gladstone And Unionists; Walter MacDonald.}   34

Miscellany
{Solow; Cullen; Lenin On Land Tenure; Feudalism? Two Kinds Of Capitalist Development.}   56

Theories Of Capitalist Development
{Thievery And Progress; R.R. Kane; Plunkett And The Catholic Church; Mediaevalism.}   62

The South 1800-1850
{Fintan Lalor: The Prophet Of Southern Capitalism; *Appendix:* "Men Of No Property"?}   70

Partition
{Catholic Nationalism; The Industrialisation Of Ulster; Home Rule And Unionism; Sinn Fein And Partition.}   77

[continues overleaf]

A Note On The First Edition 91

Summary 95

Postscript: On Small Commodity Production And Merchants' Capital
{A Criticism (Of Sorts); On General Truth Which Is Independent Of The Particular; Marx On The Appearance Of TheCapitalist In History; Marx On The Merchant And The Small Producer; Lenin On The Small Commodity Producer; The Matter Of Fact; Belfast And The Slave Trade; Nationality And The International Market.} 95

Bibliography 104

Index 105

Introduction

This is not an academic work. It evolved amidst the intense political turmoil of West Belfast in 1969-72. Though now acquiring the respectable form of a book, it has been out and about in the world in a way that not many books have been. It has been closely ready by thousands of people who would never have read it if it had in the first instance appeared as a book, even though reading it requires much more attention than most books.

The Economics Of Partition began as a magazine article in 1967. In January 1969, this article, with some additional material, was issued as a pamphlet. A second edition followed in November 1969, and a third in January 1971. Many amendments and additions were made in each of these editions but, as I do not have copies of them, I cannot indicate what the changes were. A fourth edition, greatly extended and comprehensively recast, was issued in May 1972. This was retyped on a larger page for a 1974 edition, but was apparently not changed in any other way. A number of reprints were later made from the 1974 plates, the print becoming more blotted each time. The copy from which this book was made is barely readable in parts.

I have no real idea how many copies of it have been produced in total: certainly 5,000; possibly twice that number.

All previous editions were published by the British & Irish Communist Organisation (B&ICO) without an author's name. I wrote them, but I did not do so by way of being an author. I wrote drafts for discussion and they were discussed, often very fiercely. The B&ICO in its prime was anarchist, rather than democratic centralist in structure. It had no committees for deciding important matters. Whenever a committee was set up nobody took any heed of it. Orderly structures were approved of in principle, but not tolerated in practice. It had no wealthy patrons, either native or foreign. It had no source of funds beyond the subscriptions of its members, who were chiefly manual workers, with some clerical workers, and a few professionals. It was egalitarian to an extent that nobody who did not experience it would have thought possible. Its members were so disputatious that the wonder was that it survived its own meetings. Nothing but the brute force of reason made any impression on it. And its political environment was the collapse of a state.

This book is a product of those circumstances. I doubt that anything like it could have occurred in more conventional circumstances. And I know for certain that if I had set up as an author, as people who write books usually do, I would have written nothing like it.

This is a history of Ireland from the 17th century until Partition, written in terms of Marxist political economy. But I think that the collapse of Marxism in recent years leaves it unaffected. What the B&ICO took seriously in Marxism was its political economy, and Marx's political economy was a continuation and development of classical political economy as expounded by Ricardo.

The reader will encounter the term "revisionism" throughout this book. It refers to the revising of Marxist political economy around 1960 by the Communist Parties which took their lead from Moscow. In place of the hard, objective categories which

Marx took from capitalist political economy, a sort of wishful thinking was introduced. In order to appreciate this wishful thinking, you had to become a "creative Marxist". Creative Marxism was a conjuring trick. Conjurors used to be called Illusionists. And what creative Marxists created was certainly illusion. Their castles in the air all fell down at a mere touch a year or two ago. But that has nothing to do with the B&ICO, which pointed out twenty five years ago that all they were was castles in the air.

Wassily Leontief, the foremost economic theorist of American capitalism in the fifties, said that if you wanted to know about capitalism, you should read the three volumes of Marx's "Capital". The Thatcherite ideologists would have done well to heed that advice, because they obviously thought money-changing was capitalism.

This book is all about capitalism in Ireland. The only Marxist works cited in it are Marx's Capital and Lenin's Development Of Capitalism In Russia. This is Marxism as a rounded out form of Ricardo, who in his turn was a systematic form of Adam Smith.

The creative Marxists discarded what was sound in Marx, while developing other aspects of his writing into a comprehensive, but unrealistic, philosophy. In Russia and Eastern Europe they put a straitjacket on society. In Britain a generation of them went into the Labour Party and, in leading positions, disabled it.

While Marxism could be regarded as consisting basically of political economy, I considered myself a Marxist. In the late sixties, other features of Marxism were elaborated into a dogmatic philosophy—I do not think it would be extravagant to say a theology—by Louis Althusser. Althusserian Marxism became immensely fashionable in the seventies. It formed a common ground between Moscow-line Communists and their traditional enemies, the Trotskyists; and the Labour Party newspaper, Tribune, was hardly intelligible unless you were au fait with Althusserian language. And as Marxism ceased to be primarily political economy, I ceased to consider myself a Marxist. In the late seventies I published, in The Communist, a long review of the writings of Althusser demonstrating, to my own satisfaction at any rate, that they were a form of lunacy. Since then I have considered myself to be definitely not a Marxist.

People of various dispositions could participate in B&ICO discussions because its Marxism consisted of political economy. Political economy, being a well established means of comprehending the world from a generally accessible viewpoint, requires no special belief. It is what is least like religion.

Marxist groupings proliferated in the mid-sixties. The B&ICO (for the first few years it was called the ICO) was the only one which took Marxism to be essentially political economy. No special belief was required for participation in its discussions, only a sense of reality. But a sense of reality—by which I do not mean business acumen—has been in short supply in recent times.

The B&ICO was always a very small group. It never had more than fifty members. And it never had any financing—its publishing was always done by self-help. Yet it generated waves of ideas which are still spreading around society. I have frequently had the experience of hearing very respectable people—Labour MPs let us say—condemning the B&ICO because somebody has told them to, while reciting ideas—about Labour Party organisation in Northern Ireland, let us say—

which would never have entered their heads but for the B&ICO.

The Marxist tendencies founded on belief all became very much bigger than the B&ICO, but they made no impact on people who did not share in their particular belief.

The great conflict between Marxism and the outlook of the capitalist world, which seems to have opted for the name of Liberalism, has presumably ended with the collapse of the Marxist states. Over thirty years ago, those states jettisoned what was sound in Marxism and they have been stagnant ever since. But the capitalist world which has now emerged triumphant has emerged mentally impoverished from the conflict.

Political economy was the Marxist inheritance from capitalism in its prime. Thirty-odd years ago, Marxism cast political economy aside, but the capitalist world did not take it back. Political economy is now extinct, and capitalism in its second innings is without adequate means of thought.

Political economy is not business economics. And business economics without a framework of political economy has no bearings.

Political economy takes the economy, the society and the state as an interconnected organism and analyses its physiology. It was developed chiefly by William Petty, Adam Smith, David Ricardo, and John Stuart Mill. Margaret Thatcher imagines that she revived the capitalist world outlook, but her statement that "there is no such thing as society, only individual men and women and their families", and of course their *choices*, demonstrates by its profound ignorance how badly the capitalist world outlook has been damaged.

Political economy as an academic form has all but disappeared. Insofar as rudiments of it survive, they seem to take the name of Geography.

The B&ICO discarded its Marxist trappings many years ago—long before the collapse of the Marxist states in Russia and Eastern Europe. Its Belfast Branch changed its name to the Ingram Society, after the late 19th century political and social theorist, John Kells Ingram, best known for his poem, **Who Fears To Speak Of '98?**

The B&ICO might be seen as the final fling of political economy. That is what makes its Marxist literature unique and keeps it in demand.

The copyright of all that material has been made over to Athol Books, and this is the first of a series of reprints.

It is reprinted with only a few minor changes, the chief of which is that "bourgeois" has been changed into "capitalist" in many instances, particularly where the reference is to the rural economy. And a couple of pages on the agricultural economy in the South of Ireland in the 18th century and the early 19th have been summarised down to a couple of paragraphs (pages 70-1). And some notes have been added in square brackets.

Economic determinism was heavy in the atmosphere of Belfast in the late sixties and early seventies, so I expected to find The Economics Of Partition saturated with it, even though I always tried to make ample allowance for cultural facts. I was pleasantly surprised to find so little of it. And In fact I recalled that Michael Farrell had dismissed the pamphlet as non-Marxist, because it was not economic determinist. But then, political economy did make ample allowance for non-economic factors. It is the trivial "Economics" which in recent times displaced political economy that gave rise to the simplistic economic determinist view of life which Margaret Thatcher borrowed from creative Marxism.

Finally, I should say a word about the Two Nations theory, which is what the Economics of Partition was about. When the B&ICO first put forward that theory and produced evidence to show its basis in reality, at a time when the Catholic nationalist military/diplomatic offensive against Northern Ireland was at its height and appeared on the point of success, it was met with derision, hostility and disbelief in Catholic nationalist Ireland. The group was abused as "Orange Socialist", and even described as "fascist". Its members were ostracised by the left in Britain and in Ireland—the left which over the past six or seven years has suffered moral collapse, swinging round to right wing gimmickry, and bringing the British Labour Party to the brink of ruin. The B&ICO had the moral backbone—some might say the arrogance—to follow through on its own understanding of the situation. It was the first Irish group in modern times to take a stand on conviction against the comfortable nationalist consensus.

As the evidence for the existence of the Two Nations built up, and the arguments against nationalism struck their mark, the idea gradually began to gain ground that the Unionism of the Ulster Protestant community was not an artificial creation of Tory Party policy, but was a consistent outcome of the history of that community, and of its development through popular struggle over many generations. Nowadays, the idea of the Two Nations is commonplace, though the most conservative of the nationalists still prefer to talk about two "communities" or two "traditions". But while this basic idea took off, the prejudice against the group which made it functional has persisted. It is therefore only right that the piece of historical description and reasoning which put the Two Nations theory beyond serious dispute should be made available to a new generation of readers by Athol Books.

Brendan Clifford
May, 1992

Preface To 4th Edition.

"Whenever a social mass phenomenon is ascribed to a mere stupidity of the men participating, this apparent stupidity is merely the stupidity of the observer and critic, who evidently has not succeeded in finding his bearings among conceptions and opinions foreign to him, or in penetrating to the material conditions and motives underlying these modes of thought." (K, Kautsky: **Foundations Of Christianity**.)

Those words are particularly applicable to the attitude of a section of 'the left' towards the behaviour of the Ulster Protestant masses since 1886. That section of 'the left' which came under the influence of the Catholic bourgeois nationalist view of the matter, propounded a theory elaborated on the notion that the Protestant masses were stupid bigots. The intense energy which they displayed in the Unionist cause was put down to stupidity. The general view was that they were the stupid (though highly energetic) lackeys of the feudal remnants in Ulster, notwithstanding that they included as their most vigorous element, a large industrial working class with an impressive record of trade union activity.

Some tried to conjure up an appropriate material interest for these masses in the form of imperialist bribery. The "stupid dupes" of the Orange Order were said to be a labour aristocracy defending their bribes. But this notion couldn't bear very much comparison with reality. You would need to be very much lost to this world in order to be able to feel, in the Shankill and its environs, that you were in the stronghold of an entrenched labour aristocracy. To cope with this, it was asserted that the Protestant working class was not really a labour aristocracy, but that it had been led by imperialists to believe that it was. Which, of course, made out the Protestant workers to be more stupid than ever.

The Nationalist 'left' could construct no theory to account for all the main features of the existing reality. If a theory seemed to account for one feature, it came into contradiction with another. The various pieces of the structure wouldn't dovetail. Therefore there arose a curious phenomenon. The main theoretical achievement of a Maoist existentialist group known as the Internationalists (who came and went in Ireland in the late sixties), was to elaborate this curious phenomenon into a system and give it an apt title: "theoretical pluralism".

The gist of theoretical pluralism is that, where no acceptable theory can be found which accounts for the entire situation being investigated, without conflict with the interest or prejudice of the investigating party, the various aspects of it can be explained by mutually contradictory theories. Numerous examples of theoretical pluralism are to be found in the literary heritage of anti-Partitionism. One of the most curious is that which defends the notion that there is one all-embracing Irish nation, and refutes the two Irish nations theory, by arguing that the Ulster Protestant community is not a separate nation at all, but is an integral part of the *British* nation. The part of this particular argument which says that the Ulster Protestants do not constitute a nation is alone taken account of. The part which conflicts with the one Irish nation theory is not taken account of.

These contortions are necessary only because certain false conceptions of the situation are held to be sacred, and are defended at all costs. In fact, the problem of the Unionist behaviour of the Protestant workers only appears as a problem because of these false conceptions. On the basis of the dogma that one national society with a unified national economy existed in Ireland; that national interest, democratic reform, and economic development required separation from Britain and economic protectionism; and that the Protestant workers, for no good reason, placed themselves in opposition to economic and political progress, there is a problem—and an inexplicable one. But, if there were two nations, and two economies, and those economies had conflicting requirements relative to the British market as a consequence of which Unionism made as much economic and political sense in one as Nationalism in the other, then the behaviour of the Protestant workers is no longer a difficult problem requiring theoretical pluralism to explain it.

The B&ICO decided to work out a theory of the situation which was derived objectively from the facts of the situation as a whole, and which therefore explained its essential features. Two points were reached at which the theory that was emerging from the objective investigation of the facts came into conflict with certain fundamental preconceptions with which we had been operating. The first was that Partition had not arisen despite the economic unity of North and South, but was, on the contrary, based on an economic conflict between the requirements of large-scale industry in the North and the small manufactures of the South with relation to the British market. That point was effectively dealt with in the first edition of **The Economics Of Partition**.

Proceeding from there, we investigated the political history of Partition and came very sharply up against the second preconception: that society in Ireland constituted a single, integrated, historically evolved nation. The previous edition of The Economics Of Partition still retained that preconception, which invalidated its political economy.

The present edition is entirely re-written. The political comment is brought into line with political reality. Much secondary material from previous editions has been omitted as being more relevant to the political history of Partition which the B&ICO is in process of publishing. The political economy has been greatly expanded. Only one section from the previous edition (i.e., Economics & Partition) has been retained (with revisions). This was first published in The Irish Communist in June 1967. (Previous editions of The Economics Of Partition were: 1st—January 1969; 2nd—November 1969; 3rd (with attention drawn to irresponsible politics)—January 1971.)

This pamphlet is not an economic history of Ireland, but an attempt to depict the general background of political economy to the partition conflict.

May, 1972.

Economics And Partition

"Partition arises out of this uneven development of capitalism in Ireland sentiment won't remove it." (Peadar O'Donnell. **An Phoblacht** 7.2.1931.)

Partition has dominated Irish politics for close on fifty years. If the working class is to act in its own interest in any situation, it must have a thorough understanding of that situation. Wishful thinking will get it nowhere. A large part of the understanding of the Irish situation is an understanding of Partition. Until the working class works out an understanding of the real causes of Partition, it will be befuddled by the bourgeois explanations of it.

The explaining of Partition cannot be avoided or by-passed. Numerous attempts have been made to by-pass it. The Socialist Party Of Ireland, for example, issued a manifesto in 1950 which said in effect: "To hell with all bourgeois politics and all talk about Partition. The workers on the south of the border are exploited just the same as those in the North. Let's have a movement of all the Irish workers against all the Irish bosses". Spirited words! But where is the SPI today? Where is last winter's snow?

Partition and the politics of Partition exist. They will not be overcome by a pretence that they do not exist. They will not be overcome by slogans, no matter how stimulating the slogans are, or how loud they are shouted. There is only one way in which the Irish working class can free itself from the bourgeois influence of the politics deriving from Partition—and that is by a thorough understanding of the economics and politics of Partition.

The working class has only two weapons in its fight to abolish capitalism; theory and organisation. And the working class cannot act in such a way as to further its own class interest unless it has a clear understanding of the situation it exists in. While it re-acts more or less unconsciously to developments in the bourgeois system, the system will remain. It is only when it acts on the basis of a clear understanding of the bourgeois system, and of the *peculiarities* of the system in the national situation in which it finds itself, that it acts towards putting an end to the bourgeois system. That is why Marx said that the working class is the most theoretical class in all of history.

The Irish situation includes Partition and the rival bourgeois ideologies and politics of Partition. Since 1922 workers on both sides of the border have *wished for* a united working class political movement despite Partition. But the socialist movement failed to make a scientific historical analysis of Partition, and therefore it remained subject to bourgeois nationalist divisions which Partition expressed. The greater the pressure of bourgeois ideology, the more the objective situation needs to be understood in order to develop working class politics. But the Irish working class remained dominated by the bourgeois politics of Partition. While this state of affairs continued the only united movement that could develop was one that resulted from bourgeois politics: from changes in relations between Ulster capitalism and 26 County capitalism. And, since the two bourgeoisies have remained in conflict over Partition, so have the workers in both communities.

Tactics & Taxes What is the internal basis of Partition in Ireland? Sometimes we are told that Partition is entirely the result of "Tory policies". Well, it was legislated by a Liberal Prime Minister and was guaranteed by the British Labour Party in 1949. But, whether it was Tory, Liberal or Labour politics that legislated it, there must have been some *internal* basis for it in Irish society. If there was no internal basis for it, it could not have been sustained for fifty years. Was the internal basis religious or racial? If its foundation had been either religion or race, the Partition would have been a very unstable structure. And it has not been that.

Desmond Greaves (leader of the "Connolly Association", a front organisation of the British Communist Party), gives this explanation of the basis of Partition in the British revisionist theoretical magazine, **Marxism Today** (April 1966). Home Rule, he says, would have meant that Ireland would have had to bear the cost of Irish social services and the cost of buying out the landlords.

"Clearly any government in Dublin would require to raise considerable revenue. How was this to be done? The national bourgeoisie replied by protective tariffs which would also encourage Irish industry. This Britain refused to concede. The alternative was inevitably a tax on industry for the benefit of agriculture. The most vigorous current of taxable production lay in the industrial north-east. Here also was a predominantly Protestant working class occupying a privileged position in relation to the Catholics. 'We will not have Home Rule', said the captain of industry, thinking about his taxes, and proceeded to organise the Protestant workers under the slogan of 'Home Rule is Rome Rule, so defend your privileges'."

The basis of the opposition by the Orange bourgeoisie to Home Rule was that it would mean higher taxes. The essence of the Ulster Unionist movement was a campaign to keep taxes down!

Peadar O Donnell's remark on Partition stands out a mile from this kind of balderdash, and brings us into the world of reality (though O Donnell, unlike Greaves, has never claimed to be a Marxist). "Partition arises out of the uneven development of capitalism in Ireland: sentiment won't remove it."

The "uneven development of capitalism in Ireland" refers to the fact that a modern industrial capitalism developed in the North in the course of the 19th century, while in the South capitalist industry *declined*. Ulster was viewed as the industrially *backward* part of Ireland up to the end of the 18th century, and the south was the centre of manufacturing capitalism.

The major historian of the linen industry writes: "Manufacture in the southern provinces... was nearly always worked on capitalistic lines". In Ulster, linen manufacture was a peasant industry which sprawled all over the countryside. "It would seem natural that the southern manufacture, designed for greater efficiency, elimination of waste, and better distribution of risk, should be more successful and more permanent than the ill-organised industry of Ulster". (C. Gill, **The Rise Of The Irish Linen Industry**, pp78 and 133).

Yet, at the end of the 18th century and the early 19th, the capitalist industries of the south declined (except for Guinesses), while the "ill-organised industry of Ulster" grew into a modern capitalist industry. This change was not the result of any government policies. Nearly all the government grants went to the southern industries. Nor was the change a result of the Union of 1801. The politicians of the southern middle class held that the Union *was* the cause of the destruction of southern industry. To this view, Connolly said:

"Please explain the process by which the removal of Parliament from Dublin to London to Dublin—a removal absolutely unaccompanied by any legislative interference with Irish industry—prevented the Irish capitalist class from continuing to produce goods for the Irish market? ...But neither O'Connell nor any of his imitations have ever yet attempted to analyse and explain the process by which those industries were destroyed." (**Labour In Irish History**, Chapter VI.)

And Connolly explained that:

"...the Act of Union was made possible because Irish manufacture was weak, and consequently, Ireland had not an energetic capitalist class to prevent the Union... Not that the loss of the Parliament destroyed Irish manufacture, but that the decline of Irish manufacture... made possible the destruction of the Irish Parliament." (p30.) "A native Parliament may have hindered the subsequent decay as an alien Parliament may have hastened it, but in either case, under capitalistic conditions, the process itself was as inevitable as the economic evolution of which it was one of the most significant signs." (p27.) (It is notable that Desmond Greaves writes in his biography of Connolly that Connolly's view of Grattan's Parliament was wrong. The bourgeois economist, George O'Brien, he says, "correctly identified Connolly's weak point." (p196, **The Life & Times Of James Connolly**.)

Here we can see the difference between an opportunist 'socialist' and an honest bourgeois (a rare thing these days). The only serious scientific work on the development of capitalism in Ireland is The Rise Of The Irish Linen Industry by Conrad Gill (1925). This work substantiates Connolly's conclusions with regard to Grattan's Parliament and the Union. But the Marxist, Greaves, has, in the interests of peddling his De Valeraite nonsense today, to put it out that Connolly was wrong with regard to Grattan's Parliament.

Amateur Capitalists Capitalism in the South in the second half of the 18th century was a mere bubble on the surface of the society. The capitalists had not clawed their way up from the peasantry and the urban petty-bourgeoisie, as had the English capitalists. They existed on top of a society that had not produced them. Their social base was in England. Very often they were 'public-spirited' landowners. Else they were merchants whose capital was got in England (or in the position of middlemen in the import-export trade). "Manufacture in the South was too much the work of amateurs." (Gill, p135.)

One effect of this state of affairs was described by Stephenson, an enterprising Dublin capitalist, who toured Ireland a number of times and acted as the Irish Cobden. He complained that:

"If a manufacturer wants to engage in any new branch of the linen manufacture, there must first be a consultation among the weavers to know if they will allow him to carry it into execution; for in the southern provinces they are to a man sworn into a combination to support a bill of prices they have made."

The gentleman capitalists of the south were faced with a vigorous trade union movement, and they didn't quite know what to do about it. Their predicament was described in this way by a bourgeois economist:

"Irish workmen... perhaps to a greater degree than those of Great Britain, showed themselves hostile to the adoption of labour-saving machinery... Even in England there were riots directed against the use of machinery, and the reform... was carried by the high hand of the employers. In Ireland this class was weaker and less capable of facing the struggle. Even to this day (1920) it is difficult in southern Ireland to introduce labour-saving machinery into an existing business." (D.A. Chart, **Economic History Of Ireland**, 1920, p122.)

Employers

"were left with the choice of paying higher wages than the industry would bear; allowing weavers to spend part of their time in agriculture; or paying low wages, having frequent disputes with the workers, and probably losing them altogether in a short time... The third was often adopted with disastrous consequences." (Gill, p134.)

But whichever of the three was adopted would have led to the ruin of the centralised capitalism of the South. As Connolly said, "under capitalistic conditions, the process itself was... inevitable."

Peers And Peasants   The capitalists of the south were gentlemen and their enterprises were centralised and heavily subsidised. In the north, the linen industry was carried on by peasant weavers scattered throughout the countryside. The linen found its way to Dublin through a complex of fairs. In the early stages of the journey to Dublin it was bought and sold by small scale jobbers and drapers. Every peasant weaver was the seed of a manufacturing capitalist. Every two-penny-half-penny trader was the germ of a merchant capitalist. Over a period of about a century, a solid bourgeois class was developed out of these seeds by a process of natural selection. They fought one another tooth and claw. Many were driven down into the proletariat. Luck, cunning and ruthlessness—the law of the jungle—made capitalists out of a few. And, when a "healthy" basis for trade had developed, Or, as a bourgeois would put it:

> "That remarkable growth was mainly due to private enterprise working against many difficulties" (Gill, p81). "When a class of manufacturing employers appeared in Ulster it came as a normal and healthy development, due to increased trade." (p134.)
>
> "...the manufacturing class was recruited from above and from below—from traders as well as from craftsmen" (p149).

The whole of Ireland was subject to the same laws and the same material conditions, and Northern industry was discriminated *against* in the granting of subsidies. What is the basic reason why an industrial capitalism developed in the North, but not in the South? It is the difference in the system of land tenure. In the South, the bulk of the peasants were rack-rented. Any increase in the output of a holding was followed by an immediate increase in rent. For the peasant there was no possibility of accumulating even a small stock of capital. He had no reason to produce anything more than his rent and the means of subsistence for himself and his family. Any extra production would immediately be turned into an increase in rent. The rent would be consumed by the landlord, and by the various layers of tenantry that lay between him and the peasant producer.

It made little difference to the system whether the landlord was a 'progressive', who stayed in Ireland, or a dissolute absentee in London. The land system made productive investment in the South of Ireland impossible. The efforts of a number of 'progressive' landlords in the 18th century were all brought to nothing by the land system.

In the North, the system known as "Ulster Custom" developed. Ulster custom was not a gift from the Northern landlords to their tenants. It was, as every system is, a product of historical conditions and struggle. The Ulster peasants won tenant right in struggle against the landowners. This led to an improvement in the value of the land. Once the system had been established, it would not even have been in the interests of the landowners to revert to the system of rack-renting.

In the course of the later 17th and 18th centuries, there developed in Ulster a peasant-based linen industry which was combined with agriculture. In 1770, an economic crisis knocked out many of the capitalist industries of the South. In the North, it only meant that the weavers spent more time on agriculture. The capitalist class in the North developed gradually, in what might be called a 'natural' way. After 1820, it began to apply modern industrial methods to linen production. (Linen was the 'growth' industry.) In 1830, Derry became the pioneer of the ready-made shirt industries. In 1850 the ship-building industry was started.

The Economic Foundation Of The Border The backbone of the Northern capitalist class was an industrial system. But, in the South, after the collapse of the 18th century capitalism, the bourgeoisie were what is called 'compradores'. They were distributing agents for imports from Britain. They were likely to have capital invested industrially in any part of the British Empire except Ireland. (Southern Irish capital was invested in the development of the Ruhr.)

It is clear from this that the only real large-scale industrial capitalism which has ever developed in Irish society is the capitalism of the North. This capitalism developed out of Irish society, but not mainly on the basis of the Irish home market. The market which developed it was the British market. It was hatched out of Irish society by the British market. Having developed on this basis, it could only continue to exist on this basis. It could find no basis for existence in the Irish home market.

In the South, the middle class nationalist movement which developed during the 19th century relied on production of the home market to develop manufacture in the South. Manufacture in the South required a protected home-market to facilitate its development. The policy of protectionist Home Rule was given its clearest expression by Griffith in 1905 (though it was part of the Home Rule movement for decades before that.)

This diametrical conflict of interests, resulting from the different stages of development of capitalism in the North and the South, was the foundation on which the Border was erected. "Partition arises out of this uneven development of Capitalism in Ireland". In the light of this solid reality what can one do but laugh at Greaves' 'tactical' explanation of it as part of a campaign for lower taxes in the North?

"Sentiment won't remove it". Since it has its basis in a real conflict of class interest, it will only be removed on the basis of real class interest. In 1920, the two parts of Ireland would *not* fit together to make a harmoniously functioning *bourgeois* system. No amount of cunning would make protection serve the interests of the northern capitalists. The two could not be fitted together in a system of production for profit, in which the market is all-important. They had conflicting interests in the market.

Ulster Custom

Origin The historical origin of Ulster Custom, like everything else which relates to Partition, is the subject of dispute between the historians of the rival nationalisms. In Ireland, history is propaganda. The historical propaganda of Catholic nationalism cannot admit that anything good ever came to Ireland through Protestant Ulster. But it is generally known that, in the mid-19th century, the agrarian movement in the South was demanding the extension of Ulster Custom to the South, and that substantial tenant-right had existed in the area of the Ulster Plantation for a considerable period prior to that.

How did it come about that tenant-right got established in Protestant Ulster before it came into being in Gaelic, Catholic Ireland? The simple explanation— that the Protestant tenant-farmers acquired coherence as a class, and forced the landlords to recognise tenant-right through class struggle, before the Catholic peasantry did so—is ruled out of order. Three alternatives to this view are

frequently presented:
1. There was no substantial difference between tenant-right in Ulster and elsewhere, and the view that there was is mere Unionist propaganda. (This is a pretty rarefied and sophisticated argument, and for that reason is not very popular.)
2. Ulster tenant-right was established through landlord/tenant class collaboration. The landlords *allowed* their tenants easy terms in order to divide them from the Catholic peasantry.
3. Ulster Custom had its origin in the Gaelic clan system, which survived in Ulster until the Plantation. The Planters learned the Custom from the clansmen, and managed to preserve it when it was destroyed elsewhere. (When it is asked why they managed to preserve it when the people who originated it failed to preserve it, the answer is usually in terms of the catastrophic effect of the Penal Laws on the Catholics on the one hand, and the Orange Ascendancy collaboration of landlord and tenant on the other.)

Desmond Greaves, the chief strategist of revisionism, takes the line that Ulster Custom evolved from the clan system.

A curious phenomenon is the contradictory position taken by the two revisionist Parties in their Party programmes published in 1963. (These two parties have since merged into the Communist Party of Ireland, and the new Party maintains that the two old Parties maintained a close collaboration. The two Party Programmes were certainly issued in co-ordination. And the new Party retains *both* of the Programmes*.)

According to the Irish (26 County) Workers' Party (IWP) Programme, **Ireland Her Own**:

"The division of Ireland is the result of imperialist policies. Every county has within it people of different religions and with difference ancestries. What has happened in North-East Ireland is that these differences were played on by British imperialism... Along with the political campaign to divide Ireland, went an economic policy of *allowing* more industry to develop in the North than in the rest of the country, and *giving* the Ulster tenants more rights on the land than were known in the rest of the country." (p15/6, our emphasis.)

But when we turn to the Communist Party Of Northern Ireland (CPNI) Programme we are told:

"The history of the north-eastern part of Ireland in the 18th century is one long struggle against the Crown and Aristocrats by the farming and artisan classes, resulting in a partial victory over the latter [the meaning is obviously 'over the *former*'—ed.], by the establishment of a limited form of tenant-right. This deprived the landlords of the power to evict the tenant without compensation... The Ulster Land War was the dress rehearsal for the Irish Land War of a century later.

"The Volunteer Movement of 1782 was firmly entrenched in the ideals and aspirations of the Northern Democrats and won from the British

---

* The Communist Party of Ireland was divided in 1941, following the German invasion of Russia. The Northern part, calling itself the Communist Party, Northern Ireland, supported the British war effort, along with the British Communist Party, and it fought the 1945 election on a Unionist programme. The Southern part, not being prepared to oppose De Valera's neutrality policy, called itself nothing for a while, but in the fifties it called itself the Irish Workers' Party. The two came together again in 1970 as the Communist Party of Ireland.

Government the Independence of the Irish Parliament. This independence gave the first great impulse to the growth of manufacture and trade, previously throttled by British Laws, and laid the basis for the development of much of our industry in the North" (p1/2).

So the Southern revisionist view, reflecting the propaganda of Southern bourgeois nationalism, is that the Ulster tenants were *allowed* tenant-right, and that Ulster was *given* industry by the British ruling class, acting on the policy of 'divide and rule'. But the Northern revisionist view is that tenant right was won through class struggle against the ruling class, and that the development of industry was also brought about by the struggle of popular forces against the British administration. The position of the CPNI is infinitely nearer the historical truth than that of the IWP, but would not be approved of in Catholic nationalist circles. And the IWP position would not be acceptable in the Ulster Protestant community (which was the main base of the CPNI in 1963, though it is no longer). Hence the evolution of contradictory explanations.

The Peoples' Democracy* asserts that "the relatively favourable land tenure arrangements for settlers allowed the development of a vigorous and independent class of tenant farmers" (M. Farrell. Northern Star, No. 5, p22).

The Trotskyist International Socialism group asserts:

"in the north east there has been a greater development of industry... In part this was due to official encouragement given by the British ruling class to the creation of a stable middle class. This was achieved by assisting the Protestant peasantry, descendants of the Ulster settlers in the previous century, to buy their holdings. This occurred more than 120 years before the Catholic peasants in the rest of Ireland" (**International Socialism**, April/June 1972, p15).

The more 'socialist' Catholic nationalism becomes, the nearer it approaches a total disregard for historical fact. The assertion that the Ulster Protestant peasantry were assisted in buying their holdings 120 years before the Catholics has absolutely no basis in historical fact. Government schemes for the establishment of peasant proprietorship were not introduced until the end of the 19th century, and they made no distinction between Protestant and Catholic. In fact, it was mainly in response to the pressure of the Catholic tenants movement, that the schemes for peasant proprietorship were introduced. And the Protestant tenant-farmers were certainly *not* assisted in buying their holdings in the 18th century. On the contrary,

---

* The Peoples' Democracy was a radical student movement which in 1968/9 played a critical role in the transition of the Civil Rights movement into an anti-Partitionist movement. It briefly published a theoretical magazine called the Northern Star, which has no connection with the Northern Star currently being published. The PD was intensely Marxist, loosely within the ambit of the more or less Trotskyist International Socialism (IS) group. IS, the most middle class of all the "revolutionary socialist" ideological groups, now calls itself the Socialist Workers' Party (or Movement, in Ireland). Its particular variant of revolutionism is eminently compatible with advancing one's career in the public institutions of a state which its rhetoric depicts as tending towards fascism. Its adherents include John Palmer, European Correspondent of The Guardian; Eamonn McCann, a 'personality' on BBC Radio Ulster; and John Gray, Librarian at the Linenhall Library, Belfast.

The PD disintegrated in 1970/71. Some joined the B&ICO. Those under IS influence became increasingly nationalist. The IS declared "unconditional but not uncritical" support for the IRA. The PD in its socialist phase had expressed a vigorous hostility towards C.D. Greaves and his "two-stage theory" of revolution, i.e., first the nationalist revolution then the socialist. But when it became nationalist it issued a formal announcement that it accepted the two-stage theory.

persistent efforts were made to deprive them of the *tenant-right* which they had. Could it be that these 'Marxists' don't know the difference between tenant-right and land-ownership?

Clansmen And Tenants The notion that Ulster Custom originated in the Ulster clan system is put forward by C.D. Greaves in his pamphlet, **Wolfe Tone And The Irish Nation** (Connolly Association, 1963):

"...such was the resilience of the old society that a further compromise had to be come to. The right of the kinsmen in the common land was so deeply ingrained that it was, so to speak, resurrected under the new conditions of tenancy. It became a claim to ownership with tenancy and in one of its forms became famous as 'Ulster Custom'. It was widely held that this was brought to Ireland by Scottish settlers, as it was certainly preserved by the growth of the linen industry. But it is of native Irish growth. It seems to have survived longest in Ulster because there the clans were longest preserved. Elsewhere it was lost and regained, lost and fought for again, under the title of the 'good old modus' and its interest, theoretically speaking, is that an extinguished kinship right seems to have reappeared as a capitalist right, the claim by the tenant to a disposable goodwill in his tenancy, described sometimes as a 'joint ownership'." (p6.)

And on page 10 Greaves refers to "Ulster, where the clans had survived the longest, where the tenant preserved some vestige of his ancient rights." Greaves merely asserts this. He doesn't supply a shred of evidence in support of it. He doesn't make any attempt to show *how* the Gaelic clan system had such a fundamental social influence on the Plantation peasantry, who regarded the clansmen much in the same way as the American planters of the same period regarded the Red Indian tribal organisation. Or, alternatively, he doesn't attempt to show that the Custom was enforced by clansmen who were given holdings in the Plantation Counties, and not, as is generally supposed, by the planter peasantry.

There are some very formal similarities between the clan system and the Ulster Custom system of land tenure. In addition to these very abstract similarities, it is also the case that in the years between the defeat of O'Neill's rebellion and the Ulster Plantation (from 1603 to 1610), the English administration under Chichester and Sir John Davies gave legal recognition to the rights of the clansmen, as against the chief, in the ownership of land. On a purely formal level, therefore, it would be possible to argue that the Ulster Custom system of capitalist landholding was a development of the old Ulster clan system of landholding, with Sir John Davies' legislation as the point of qualitative development between the two. But this formal gloss on history breaks down when the concrete historical process is dealt with. It is not a theory that has been hewn out of the actual historical process. It is a scheme that is projected onto history in the interests of De Valeraite propaganda.

The formal similarity between the two systems is this—the actual social relations were not reflected in the legal framework in either system. In each, there was a state of tension between the actual working population on the land and what might be termed the aristocracy. In each, the working population checked the power of the aristocracy in practice, though not by legal means.

But, while the actual rights of the tenant farmer under Ulster Custom were substantially *greater* than his theoretical legal rights, the actual rights of the clansman were substantially *less* than his theoretical legal rights. Ulster Custom carried the actual democratic rights far beyond their legal expression, through the social power of the peasantry. But, the actual rights of the working people in the clans fell far short of their theoretical extent according to law, because of the social impotence of the clansmen.

The strength and coherence of the tenant-farmers enabled them to eat into the power of the landlord. But, in the clan system, it was the chiefs who eroded the power of the clansmen.

According to the Brehon Laws, the chiefs were not the landlords of the clan lands. In fact, the chiefs established extensive private ownership for themselves, and increasingly exacted rents from the clansmen, even though the old legal framework was maintained.

In disputes over the chieftainship between members of the aristocratic families, the rival aristocrats could establish factions of clansmen to support their claims, by appealing to the ideology of the system. The clansmen could constitute the following of rival aristocrats, but they never challenged aristocracy as an independent social force as the tenant-farmers did.

Following the defeat of the O'Neill's rebellion, Chichester and Davies attempted to change the social relations in the clan system. Davies tried to evolve a new and more stable land system from the clan, which would be a development of elements already existing in that system. He held that the chiefs were not the owners of the clan lands, and sought to develop the clansmen into tenants with security of tenure, and to reduce the chief to a landlord with restricted powers over his former clansmen, who had become his tenants. If this policy had been persisted in, it may have led to something similar to Ulster Custom. In fact, it was abandoned after the Flight of the Earls, and the O'Dogherty rebellion of 1608, when the Plantation policy was decided upon.

(In Connacht, the British administration had achieved something along these lines in the "Composition of Connaught" late in the 16th century. The clansmen were evolved into tenants, and the chiefs into landlords. But the Connacht nobility were not chiefs in the proper sense. The dominant families were Norman feudal lords who had adopted a Gaelic way of life.)

George Sigerson All that Greaves gives in support of his assertion is a reference to George Sigerson's **History Of Land Tenures And Land Classes Of Ireland** (1871. This is the same person who wrote **Bards Of The Gael & Gall**). The relevant part of Sigerson seems to be the following:

"The land customs of the Scottish and Welsh settlers were, like their language, very similar to the Irish. Those customs went to the formation of what is now known as the Ulster Custom, though it existed then, so far as security of tenure is concerned, all over Ireland, except where Border-practice could rule unchecked. Did the English settlers contribute anything to the formation of this custom? We believe they contributed to shape it, by moulding the congenial native elements after their own copyhold custom, and so helped, by virtue of their ascendancy, to obtain its recognition" (p48/9).

"In reality it extended over Ireland—but in Ulster it has remained almost intact, because the political and religious causes that devastated the South, and as far as possible destroyed its ancient right and customs, did not hurt the North. The prominent Ulster tenants were Protestants, so that the province was not wasted by the Penal Laws. They retained their arms, rose in defence of their custom more than once, and did not vote against their landlords. Thus they remained undisturbed until quite recently..." (p65).

"...this custom was once general over the country... its local designation is only due to the fact that in Ulster it has been allowed to remain almost intact" (p281).

"Now what land-customs would the English tenantry carry to Ireland with them? Not those of mere villeins, for the lowest class could not go... the lowest class who could go over were copyholders, either in fact or lawful expectation" (p51).

Sigerson reviews the Tudor and Stuart Plantations in general and concludes: "The Plantation schemes of both North and South show that it was intended to exclude tenants-at-will" (p58).

What Sigerson says is not quite what Greaves attributes to him. In fact, his views are contradictory. He asserts (without demonstrating) that tenant-right derives from the clan-system, and then shows that it was the aim of all of the Plantations to develop a stable agricultural population on the basis of security of tenure. He says that, for the most part, the English settlers came from a class of copyhold tenants, who were therefore a whole historical era removed from the clansmen, and had an infinitely more developed sense of their rights as tenants. He says that the settlers "by virtue of their ascendancy" were able to maintain the ancient right when the Catholic tenantry could not, and he makes reference to "the prominent Ulster tenants". But what is significant in Ulster Custom is not the rights of "prominent tenants" (by which is meant the undertakers, presumably), but the rights of the mass of 20 acre, 10 acre and even 5 acre tenants. The term "ascendancy" has long had little precise meaning in the hands of certain Nationalist propagandists. If these small farmers are to be included within it, it becomes a mere religious term for non-Catholic (and is now frequently used as such). A great section of this small farmer 'ascendancy' (the Presbyterians) themselves came under the operation of the Penal Laws. And we will see how they were 'allowed' to preserve their tenant-right.

(Sigerson's remark that "the land customs of the Scottish... settlers, were like their language, very similar to the Irish" typifies Catholic nationalist ignorance of the history of Scotland. The Irish Celtic colonisation of the Scottish Highlands is looked back on with pride, and it is taken for granted that this was the basis of Scottish national development. In fact, the centre of national development in Scotland was not the Celtic Highlands, but the Saxon Lowlands. The social development of the Highlands was kept at a primitive level by the clan system until the 18th century. The migrants and planters who came to Ulster in the 17th century were mainly Lowland Scots of Saxon origin, whose language, religion, land system, and general world outlook were vastly different from those of Celtic Ulster and the Celtic Highlands.)

Gavan Duffy Charles Gavan Duffy, in his history of **The League Of North And South** (the tenant-right movement of 1850-54), writes:

"From the period of the Plantation of Ulster by James I, the English and Scotch planters had allowed their tenants a special tenure, which came to be known as the Ulster tenant-right... This right did not exist in the Southern provinces, but there was the root and foundation of a still clearer right. For the Southern tenants were descendants of the clans who had owned the land in common with the chiefs under native law, and who had been tricked out of their property without their knowledge or consent by the substitution of the feudal tenures for the patriarchal system. They understood their claim imperfectly indeed, but they knew that their fathers and their father's fathers had tilled the same soil, had fenced and erected whatever farm buildings it possessed at their own cost, and that the landlords sole share in the enterprise had been to draw the rent." (p25/26.)

Duffy had been actually involved in the tenants' movement with Protestant and Catholic tenant-righters, and, like the other founders of the Young Ireland movement, was a substantial bourgeois intellectual, very unlike the school of shallow Nationalist agitators that arose later in the century. He makes no attempt to link Ulster Custom with the customs of the clan system, and represents it as an original phenomenon of the Plantation society.

His statement about the custom of the clans being the "root" of tenant-right in the South is a mere piece of sentiment. He admits in the next sentence that the Southern tenant farmers did not "understand" that this was the root of their claim, and that their dissatisfaction arose not from a deprivation of past rights which they were struggling to regain, but from the actual production relations existing on the land, through which their improvements were confiscated by the landlords. (So long as the Catholic peasants' movement looked back to the clans—as it often did in the 18th century—it did so under the influence of the dispossessed clan aristocracy, and it remained a mere movement for the re-establishment of the old aristocracy.)

Montgomery One substantial historian of Irish land tenure writes that the origin of Ulster Custom

"is uncertain. But it has plainly been built up partially on rude notions of equity, and partially on a blending of the Irish notions with those of the settlers... It is possible that the Irish notions were gradually assimilated to a theory of land tenancy strongly resembling copyhold" (W.E. Montgomery, **History Of Land Tenure In Ireland**, Cambridge University, 1899, p76).

Montgomery does not attempt to show how this "blending" might have occurred through the relations of extreme hostility existing between the settlers and the native clansmen in the early period of the Plantation. It seems extremely unlikely that the Ulster settlers were influenced by "Irish notions" of land tenure (unless "Irish notions" included those of Davies and Chichester, described earlier). And, in his main section on Ulster Custom, Montgomery does not even refer to this possibility. He says:

"...it had its inception in the plantation of James I, arising not so much from the actual form of the grants then made, as from a certain sturdy self-assertiveness in the colony imported, aided by the fact that more of the landlords were resident." (p120.)

Ulster Protestant Views There was not, in the traditions of the Ulster Protestant tenants themselves, any connection between their tenant-right and the Gaelic clan system.

James M'Knight, a leader of the campaign for the legislation of Ulster tenant-right in the 1840s, and editor of the Liberal Presbyterian newspaper, **Banner Of Ulster**, published in 1848 a pamphlet called, **The Ulster Tenant-Right**. In M'Knight's view:

"The Flight of the Earls... left the native Irish without leaders, and their enormous territories... forefeited to the Crown... The premature rebellion and death of the young chief of Ennishowen, Sir Cahir O'Doherty, soon after the commencement of James' reign, greatly augmented the previous confiscations, and determined him on adopting, on a larger and more secure basis than had ever before been attempted, the policy of colonising the nation with British settlers... This was the public object to be accomplished: and as a means to that end, it was absolutely necessary, that special *beneficial* inducements should be held out to British residents, as a *premium* for their

21

settlement upon the lands of Ulster. The danger to immigrants locating themselves here was most imminent... In these circumstances... it is evident that *to induce* colonization upon large scale, there must have been strong temptations held out in the shape of *beneficial tenures of land*." (p14-15.)

J. Hancock, land agent to Lord Lurgan, giving evidence in 1844 to a Royal Commission on landlord-tenant relations (the Devon Commission) said:

"It is a system which has prevailed since the settlement of Ulster by James I, when the ancestors of many of the present landlords got grants, on condition of bringing over a certain number of sturdy yeomen and their families, as settlers. It is not likely that the patentees were wealthy... we may, therefore, fairly presume that the settlers built their own houses, and made improvements at their own expense, contrary to English practice. This, together with the fact of their being Protestants, with arms in their hands, gave them strong claims of their landlord and leader and in this way, it is probable, but it is a matter of speculation, the tenant-right may have first originated: and the Protestant settlers obtaining it in this way, it has gradually extended itself to the whole rural population of Ulster." (**Commission Report**, part 1, p483).

The same view is expressed in most Ulster Protestant historians, e.g., J.B. Woodburn, **The Ulster Scot**.

The Ulster Scot There had been a substantial movement of people from Scotland to Ulster since the 15th century. But the character of the Scots who came in the 17th century was radically different from that of the earlier migrants. A powerful revolutionary development had been taking place in the Scottish Lowlands since the mid 16th century, under the political form of the Presbyterian Reformation. And it was from a Presbyterian stronghold in the Western Lowlands that the 17th century migration came (beginning with the large private migration to Antrim an Down from 1607, followed by official Government Plantations in the rest of the province from 1610). In Scotland itself, the struggle against feudalism was prolonged. But the migration to Ulster was undertaken by the bolder spirits of the peasantry, and the entrenched institutions of feudalism with the weight of centuries behind them could not easily be transplanted. It was the democracy of Scotland that went to Ulster.

"A hoary institution of Scotland quietly disappeared from the scene in the colonization of Ulster: feudalism was not transplanted to Northern Ireland. This mark of the Middle Ages was to linger on in Scotland itself for another century, but the arrangements in Ulster, for all their superficial resemblance to Scottish land tenure, were new bargains with new men, lacking the traditional usages of feudalism." (J.G. Leyburn: **The Scotch-Irish**, 1962, p97.)

The Devon Commission Finally, we will quote the conclusions of the **Inquiry into the state of the Law an Practice in respect to the Occupation of Land in Ireland**, carried out by the Royal Commission established by the Tories in 1844, and chaired by Lord Devon. The thoroughness and objectivity of British Royal Commission Reports was commented on by Marx, and four large volumes of evidence demonstrate that the Devon Commission exerted itself to find out exactly what was happening on the land in Ireland. It was commissioned to inquire into the matter, and advise on amendments to the Law, "which having due regard to the just rights of Property, may be calculated to encourage the cultivation of the Soil, to extend the system of Agriculture, and to improve the relation between Landlord and Tenant in Ireland." In fact, the Commission was led, by the evidence it heard, to adopt an ambiguous position on the just rights of property.

It began its Report with a "slight sketch of the manner in which landed property in Ireland has been dealt with for a long series of years", and observed:

"In the civil contentions which at various periods and during many centuries disturbed the repose of England and Scotland, property gradually passed from the feudal tenure of former times to the more civilised relation of landlord and tenant, as known to our present law. It is for us briefly to show how different has been the case in Ireland" (Part 1, p6).

It held the extensive confiscations of the 17th century, and the anti-Catholic law, mainly responsible for the failure of stable landlord-tenant relations to evolve in the greater part of Ireland, and it took account of the "striking peculiarity" of property relations in Ulster. Concerning the latter, it commented:

"...the extensive settlement of Scotch and English in the counties of Ulster, has introduced habits and customs which give a different character to that province from other parts of the island. Hence also is supposed to have arisen the system of tenant-right, which, as forming a singular feature in the relation of landlord and tenant, we shall afterwards have occasion to notice. In Munster the plantation was more imperfectly carried out, and a class of undertakers, unaccompanied by those followers whom they were equally bound by the terms of their grant to introduce, became the landlords of the native peasantry in many parts of those districts, producing, for that reason comparatively little change" (p7).

The Commission's conclusions on Ulster Custom are as follows:

"In the account given by witnesses throughout Ireland, of the mode in which occupiers hold their land, the most striking peculiarity is the custom prevalent in the northern counties, called tenant-right. The origin of this custom has been the subject of much speculation, but is now rather a matter of curiosity than of present interest. It dates from a very early period, having probably sprung up as a natural consequence from the manner in which landed property was generally granted and dealt with in that part of the country.

"Large tracts having become the property of public bodies, or of individuals resident at a distance, the landlords were well contented to let their farms to those who would undertake the cultivation and entire management, reserving to themselves a rent, but making no expenditure, and exercising little interference with the land. Under such circumstances, it seems neither extraordinary nor unreasonable, that a tenant quitting his farm, either at his own desire or from some difference with his landlord, should obtain from his successor a sum of money, partly in remuneration of his expenditure, and partly as a price paid for the possession of the land which the new tenant would have no other means of acquiring.

"From this state of things a feeling of co-proprietorship appears to have grown up in the tenant, which continues in a great degree to the present day... Under the influence of this custom, the tenant claims, and generally exercises, a right to dispose of his holding for a valuable consideration, although he may have expended nothing on permanent improvements. We found that in various parts of that province, sums equal to ten, twelve, or fifteen years' purchase upon the rent, are commonly given for the tenant-right; and this not only where the rent is considered low, but where it is fully equal to value...

"Anomalous as this custom is, if considered with reference to all ordinary notions of property, it must be admitted that the district in which it prevails has thriven and improved, in comparison with other parts of the country; and although we can foresee some danger to the just rights of property from the unlimited allowance of this 'tenant-right', yet we are sure that evils more immediate, and of a still greater magnitude, would result from any hasty or general disallowance of it, and still less can we recommend any interference with it by law" (p14-15).

The observations made here on how the Custom may have evolved are very inadequate. But they demonstrate at least that the Commissioners hadn't been let in on the long term 'plot', which the British ruling class is alleged by the Catholic nationalist bourgeoisie and 'socialists' to have implemented over two and a half centuries, of "allowing" tenant right to the Protestant tenants in order to divide them from the Catholic tenants, and to achieve the uneven development of capitalism. Or perhaps the Devon Commissioners were only *pretending* not to know about this plot! Such things, at least, are imaginable by the conspiratorial petty bourgeois mind.

Development Of Tenant-Right Tenant-right was not a privilege *allowed* to an "ascendancy". It was a right *enforced* by an oppressed class. While the Plantation scheme provided for a certain security for tenants, and this was probably 'allowed' when the Plantation was actually being carried out, it was not the articles of the Plantation, or the altruism of the undertakers (or landlords) that continued and developed it over the centuries. "Rights" in the class struggle are powers. They do not exist by virtue of documents, or the liberality of the ruling classes, but by virtue of the power of the class which asserts them. The tenant-right of Ulster survived and developed because of the determination and the ability of the class of tenant-farmers to enforce it.

There is little information available on the development of landlord-tenant relations in Ulster during the 17th century. The fact that the Ulster Protestant community, particularly the Presbyterian element, was closely involved in the revolutionary movement which was overcoming the aristocracy and the absolute monarchy in Scotland and England throughout the century, would be likely to ensure that the economic position of the tenantry would not deteriorate. But, in the long period of peaceful evolution following the consolidation of bourgeois political power through the defeat of James II, the landlords tried to establish their own unconditional right to the land.

The general economic situation in Ireland was favourable to this. The mass of former clansmen throughout the country were a disorganised peasantry, incapable as yet of engaging in combined and disciplined action in support of specific capitalist demands. Despite the romancing of Greaves, the survival of clan traditions among them would not have helped them to organise themselves for winning capitalist rights on the land. The notion that "extinguished kinship right seems to have reappeared as a capitalist right" is a fantasy. The conception of capitalist right arose from capitalist conditions of existence. And it was also capitalist conditions of existence that developed the *power* of independent action in the mass of the people to enforce such rights. The clan system, as it existed in Ireland for many centuries before its abolition, smothered all power of independent action by the people.

As one of the more objective Nationalist historians puts it: "the mass of the people... were merely instruments in the hands of turbulent chiefs". And, even though there was considerable freedom in the social intercourse between chiefs and people, "it was the freedom between a master and a servant of the same family as himself on whose fidelity he knows he can rely" (Rev. E.A. D'Alton, **History Of Ireland**, Volume 1, p197-8).

The fact the Southern peasants were as yet incapable of enforcing tenant-right was a source of danger to the tenant-right of Ulster, both by way of example to the Northern landlords, and of the supply of potential tenants, who would agree to rack-rents, that it provided.

How Tenant-Right Was 'Allowed' In Ulster   In **The Ulster Land War Of 1770** (1910), F.J. Biggar, himself a Nationalist, gives the following description of how tenant-right was 'allowed' in Ulster:

"'The benefits which the undertakers secured for themselves [at the time of the Plantation] they were obliged to share with the tenants by letting the lands on the most liberal terms... The division and allotment of the lands, therefore, were not made merely that the undertakers... should become wealthy at the expense of the tenants; nor were the latter brought here to live as feudal serfs' (quoted from G. Hill: Plantation of Ulster)... Yet in a few generations we find these undertakers throwing over the whole political form by which they had been created, and dubbing themselves 'landlords'... From this their usurpation spread into a wide system of land-grabbing and rack-renting..." (p7).

The first major disturbances occurred in the 1750s, on the Donegall estates in the Belfast area that is now Legoniel (then the townland of Edenderry), when Lord Donegall tried to introduce the middleman system that was widespread in the South:

"In May 1757, John Greg of Belfast... bought by public auction the tenants' lands of Ballywalter, Ballycalcatt, and Ballykinney, in co. Antrim, from Lord Donegall. He sublet the lands, acting as middleman" (p28).

And he was confronted with agrarian terrorism.

The first tenants' movement of a general kind occurred in the 1760s in the form of the Oakboys (or Green Boys). According to Lecky (**Ireland In The 18th Century**, Volume 2):

"The Oakboys appear to have first arisen against the Road Act, which ordered that all highways should be repaired by the personal labour of housekeepers. It was stated that the landed proprietors constituted the grand juries, had many roads made which were of little or no use to the community at large, and were intended for the exclusive benefit of their own estates... In addition... the question of tithes had recently acquired in the North, as well as in the South, a new prominence... Tithes had long been paid with much reluctance in Ulster, and the clergy had often, without actual violence, been grossly defrauded of their rights. Thus it frequently happened that the farmers of a large and scattered parish, though they cut corn at different times, agreed to give notice to the clergyman that they would all draw it on the same day; and as they refused to furnish him with any horses to secure his share he was obliged to leave it on the open field, where it was sure to be wasted, spoiled or stolen, or to compound for his tithes perhaps a fourth part of the value."

"It was in the summer of 1763 that bodies of men, sometimes 400 or 500 strong, assembled to the sound of a horn, wearing oak boughs in their hats.

They erected gallows, attacked houses, compelled clergymen to swear that they would not levy more than a specified proportion of tithe, and laymen that they would not assess the county at more than a stipulated rate, entered into engagements to make no more high roads, and assaulted all whom they found working on the roads. Dr. Clark (Episcopalian Rector of Armagh) was seized and carried in derision through various parts of the country, and many of the clergy were compelled to take refuge within the walls of Derry. The flame spread rapidly through Armagh, Tyrone, Derry and Fermanagh" (p46-7).
This disturbance was ended through a combination of force and concession.

In 1771, Lord Donegall, an absentee landlord in Antrim and Down,
"when his leases fell in, instead of adopting the usual plan of renewing them at a moderate increase of rent, ...determined to raise a sum which was stated at no less than £100,00 in fines upon his tenants, and as they were utterly unable to pay them, two or three rich merchants of Belfast were preferred to them. The improvements were confiscated, the land was turned into pasture, and the whole population of a vast district were driven from their homes. This case, though the most flagrant, was by no means the only one..."
"The conduct of Lord Donegall brought the misery of the Ulster peasantry to a climax, and in a short time many thousands of ejected tenants banded together under the name of Steelboys, at first almost exclusively, Presbyterians... They attacked many houses, and were guilty of many kinds of violence, and they soon administered illegal oaths, and undertook the part of general reformers. One of their number being confined at Belfast, a large body of Steelboys, accompanied by many thousands of peasants, who neither before nor after took any part in the insurrection, marched upon that town and succeeded in obtaining his surrender" (p47-8).

A number of documents relating to this period have been published in **Aspects Of Irish Social History**, 1750-1800, by the Public Record Office of Northern Ireland (1969). One of these (written in 1772) relates:
"For five years and a half, one barony in which Lurgan is situated has paid no county cess, no constable daring to collect it. At our last assize the Grand Jury came to a resolution to have it collected by military aid...; this was made known to the land holders of the barony, upon which they assembled in a body and went to several gentlemen's houses, denouncing threats of burning their houses in case there should be an attempt made to levy the cess. As they met with no resistance they became much elated with their success, and the price of land also became a grievance... Any people who had land to set, they pulled down or burned their houses, if they refused to grant leases at twelve shillings an acre for the best and any who held land above that rate have been obliged to surrender their leases and come under oath to pay no more... Mr. Johnston of Gilford in order to show a proper discouragement to their proceedings assembled the most decent of his neighbours and had them disciplined for several days, and held them and his domestics as guard to his house." He also sallied forth and captured some prisoners. "Next day they sent him a message that if he did not deliver their men that day they would burn his house and kill himself, and to prepare for the undertaking they went into Lurgan and obliged the people there to supply them with all the guns in the town and the ammunition, and on Thursday they went to attack Mr. Johnson. On his declaring his resolution of defence, they began to fire at the windows and set the offices on fire." A clergyman in the house tried to

negotiate and was shot. "Mr. Johnson hung out a flag of truce on losing his chaplain..., and during the attempt to settle preliminaries of peace Mr. Johnson escaped out of a back window and fled on foot but was so closely pursued that he was obliged to swim the Bann and had several shots fired at him in the water." (p15.)

At the same time a lady in Portstewart was writing:

"We have bags of sand nailed up in most of our windows to keep out their balls, and plenty of charges ready made in paper, to charge the faster, and six guns always ready. Most gentlemen's houses are like garrisons: they have six soldiers and a captain at my uncle's now... The generality of the rioters were common people, labourers or tradesmen, headed by farmers, and connived at by many more... Their grievances are high rents and high markets, they pretend, especially tithes, but in reality it is thought it is only a turbulent rebellious inclination against our church or any church but the meeting house."

Seventy years later (1844) a standard question of the Devon Commission in the various localities concerned agrarian terrorism. Here are some replies taken at random from the evidence:

James Porter, Presbyterian Minister, Drumlee, Co. Down: "An attempt was made to dispossess the owner without allowing him to sell... and we were greatly scandalised by it. In fact, armies were brought in, and honest men were involved, and surprised at the violence and murderous dispositions manifested, when parties were excited about it; for I ought to state, perhaps, that every particle of improvement, every stone upon my farm, and every slate, was put together by myself, and every tree planted out of my own pocket..."

Daniel Gun Brown, Presbyterian Minister, Newtownhamilton: "it is very dangerous to meddle with what a farmer considers his right of possession. It was thought that Mr. Powell interfered in a particular case... Mr. Powell was murdered in the evening of the day".

And that is the story of how tenant-right was "allowed" by the gentry of Ulster to their tenant farmers.

As a result of these conflicts, Ulster Custom was preserved. The *certainty* that agrarian outrage would meet any attempt to infringe it made for great stability in landlord-tenant relations. As J. Hancock (Lord Lurgan's land agent) put it in his evidence to the Devon Commission:

"The landlords were compelled to recognise tenant-right; as... when they refused to allow tenant-right the incoming tenant's house has been burned, his cattle 'houghed', or his crops trodden down by night. The dis-allowance of tenant-right, as far as I know, is always attended with outrage. A landlord cannot even resume possession himself without paying for it. In fact, tenant right is one of the sacred rights of the country, which cannot be touched with impunity, and if systematic attempts were made amongst the proprietors of Ulster to invade tenant-right, I do not believe there is a force at the disposal of the Horse Guards sufficient to keep the peace in the province." (Commission Report, p484.)

Here is a respected land agent informing a Royal Commission (made up of landlords) that a blatant infringement of the ownership rights of the landlord class, enforced by agrarian terrorism, is a "sacred right of the country". He furthermore stated his agreement with it, not merely as a practical necessity, but in principle. He considered that "it is perfectly right that this tenant-right should exist", and thought it was "beneficial to the community". If it had not been made a practical necessity by the action of the tenants it would not have been conceded by the landlords. But, since it had been made a practical necessity, its capitalist virtues were recognised, especially by the land agents who tended to be very capitalist in outlook. And, as we have seen, though the Devon Commission was a bit scandalised by this state of affairs, it considered it wiser not to recommend any government interference.

"The stability of Ulster society in the 18th century depended in the last resort on the nerve of the ruling classes. Since there was no police force and the military could only be summoned in exceptional circumstances law and order was based on the support of the mass of the people" (N. Ireland, Public Record Office: Some Aspects Of Irish Social History, p42).

The mass of the people were tenant-farmers determined to enforce tenant-right, therefore the ruling class had to recognise tenant right as a prerequisite for social stability. Having to maintain its rule, without the aid of massive external force, over a vigorous class of tenant-farmers aware of its rights and determined to enforce them, the Ulster landlords of necessity had their wits about them. If they had been the "Tory backwoodsmen" of popular Nationalist mythology, Ulster society would not have developed as it did.

Davis And The Aristocracy In the 1840s Thomas Davis, reacting against the parasitic and degenerate Anglo-Irish landlord class in the South, had a vision of an ideal national aristocracy:

"A landed gentry, born and bred at home, might supply the people with an important element of peace, government and civilisation. Its young men might grow up... conversant with the working of society and trained to bodily and mental excellence. Their feelings might naturally be of equal nobility... attached by hereditary achievements to the glory of their country¬ conscious from childhood of a splendid responsibility... surrounded by the love of the many... invited by vistas of honourable distinction... such an aristocracy would give the national army officers uniting proud honour, popularity, and instruction... to the Senate men (the best of all) having a philosophical culture and ripeneing experience... Above all, it would give knowledge, union, help, advice and love to its tenantry." (Davis selection, **Thinker & Teacher**, ed. by A. Griffith, p2).

In the South, such an aristocracy seemed a Utopian vision. In the North it existed. The Northern landed gentry, kept up to scratch by a pushing tenantry threatening agrarian outrage if they wandered from the paths of righteousness, came as near to being a realisation of Davis's ideal aristocracy as is practically possible.

The "landlord backwoodsmen" notion of the Ulster aristocracy, which appears in Nationalist propaganda, is another myth. The bulk of the Southern landlords could be accurately described by backwoodsmen. They acquired bad habits by ruling over a helpless peasantry. When the peasantry ceased to be helpless, this landlord class very rapidly became helpless and useless and had to be abolished. A large section had lapsed into bankruptcy even before the peasantry rose against them as a class. As Marx observed:

"That in due course of time the [rack-renting] landlord, beside injuring the tenant will injure himself and ruin himself, is not only a probability, but the very fact, in Ireland." (**On Ireland**, p62.)

The aristocracy retained a position for itself in industrial Ulster long after it had become a despised and powerless caste in the agricultural South. This state of affairs is obviously not to be explained by the backwardness, either of the landlords, or of the general population of Ulster.

"It is clear from the Abercorn papers of the mid 18th century that the landlord and his agent had on their side to be prepared to supervise the estate carefully if they wished to safeguard and preserve their interests against the encroachments of the tenants." (**Irish Economic Documents**, HMSO, Belfast, 1967, p11.) They could not simply rake in the rack-rents, like the Southern landlords. They had to take a close interest in their own estates, and make themselves socially useful, in order to survive. Under pressure from their tenants, they became, on the whole, a very bourgeois aristocracy, much more like the British than the Southern Irish aristocracy. They developed a 'public service' tradition, not out of philanthropy (which was the only reason a Southern landlord occasionally did so), but in the interests of survival. Before the development of democratic local government authorities, many of them took the initiative in developing commercial and social amenities. For example, the Londonderry (Stewart) family, with estates in County Down, built the town of Newtownards to facilitate commercial development in the area. This same family established one of the first Volunteer companies in the 1770s, and supported the movements for legislative independence, and the electoral reform of Grattan's Parliament. In the 1790s, they had to engage in debates with their tenants, who were attracted to the United Irishmen movement. Following the suppression of the United Irishmen (unlike the Wexford aristocracy), they tried to minimise Government retaliation in order to prevent the aggravation of landlord-tenant relations.

[The two last sentences are substantially incorrect. While Lord Londonderry remained one of the better landlords economically, his political conduct was deplorable. He fostered the reform movement until 1794, changed to the reactionary side in 1795, and until 1798 urged on the Government regime of terror which led to the revolution. He punished the tenants, who had become reformers under his influence, when they declined to become reactionaries with him. And he used his influence vindictively in the North Down Courtmartials which followed the Rebellion. I have described his conduct in Introductions to reprints of James Porter's **Billy Bluff**, Steel Dickson's **Scripture Politics**, and Ledlie Birch's **Causes Of The Rebellion**, all published by Athol Books in 1991. But Londonderry's son, Castlereagh, did play a notable part in helping the new Viceroy, Lord Cornwallis, to curb Ascendancy terror in the aftermath of the Rebellion. Note to 1992 edition.]

It was because they were pressurised by their tenants into making themselves useful in the bourgeois development of society, that the Ulster aristocracy retained a leading position in society down to the mid-twentieth century.

The Political Economy Of Tenant-Right The landlord in Ulster, as elsewhere, was legally the absolute owner of the land (leaving aside the legal convention of Crown ownership). In law, the tenant had the use of the land for the duration of the lease, provided he paid his rent, and then the land reverted to the landlord to do as he pleased with. That was the law, but it was not the reality. The reality was that improvements effected on the land were the property of the tenant. And, since the original land cannot be physically separated from improvements to it, a kind of joint ownership of the land was developed.

Montgomery quotes the following definition of tenant-right by a tenant:

"Tenant-right I consider to be the claim of the tenant and his heirs to continue in undisturbed possession of the farm so long as the rent is paid; and in case of ejectment, or in the event of a change of occupancy, whether at the wish of the landlord or tenant, it is the sum of money which the new occupier must pay to the old one for the peaceable enjoyment of his holding."

He also quotes a landlord definition:

"Tenant-right is the custom under which the tenant-farmers in the north of Ireland... expect that when they have occasion to give up their farms, that their landlords will allow them to obtain from the incoming tenants such a sum as shall remunerate them for their improvements upon these farms... and for the goodwill to the farm." (p119.)

The tenants regarded the land as being theirs so long as they paid the rent; the landlord naturally did not. Rent increases were allowed for, on the condition that the rent was always a 'fair' one. And what was 'fair' naturally depended on how economic conditions affected the two parties. But a rent increase which made inroads into the value of the tenant-right would be regarded as a rack-rent, and would be ruled unconstitutional by agrarian outrage. The landlord was accorded a say in determining the price of the tenant-right, and would naturally try to keep it as low as possible. (It would not suit his interest that the part of the land which he did not own should grow in value relatively to the part which he did own.) But, in the long run, the price of the tenant-right would tend towards its market value. If the landlord put a limit to it, that limit might be formally adhered to in the official price, with money changing hands informally to make up the market-price.

A relatively free market in tenant-right developed. When a piece of land changed hands, the outgoing tenant sold the tenant-right to the incoming one as his own property. The landlord drew the rent. If the landlord wanted full possession of a farm at the expiring of a lease, he himself would have to buy the tenant-right.

Official statistics on the value of the tenant-right are, of course, not available. Montgomery (1889) says its price could be up to twenty years' purchase. In the 1840s, W.N. Hancock (see below) reckoned that tenant-right sold from 10 to 15 years' purchase, while the landlord's interest in the land sold at from 20 to 30 years' purchase. An estimate in the mid-century put its total value at £20 million.

Though it was outside the law, and ultimately dependent on the threat of agrarian outrage, the custom achieved great stability, and the tenant-right became a definite economic category, capable of being finely calculated. This indicates that it was not merely the product of an arbitrary struggle of landlord and tenant. Its political economy was explained as follows in **The Tenant Right Of Ulster Considered Economically**, published in 1845 by W. Neilson Hancock (one of the school of Ricardian political economists which flourished in Ireland in the mid-19th century):

"...an English or Scottish landlord, who lays out money on his estate, in building, fencing, and repairing, is a capitalist as well as a landlord, and the sum of money, commonly called 'rent', paid by the English or Scotch tenant is partly the profit of the capital so expended by the landlord, and partly the land-rent which he receives as a landlord...

"The Irish landlord in general never lays out any money on the improvement of his estate, so that he is not a capitalist and landlord, but a landlord only... The Irish tenant who effects whatever is done in the way of building and fencing, is not only a labourer and capitalist making investments for short periods, like the English and Scotch tenant, but is also a capitalist making investments in all the permanent improvements effected on his farm—the heir of an Irish tenant is consequently, almost always a proprietor of inherited profit, besides being a labourer and capitalist... The Irish landlord, therefore, is generally entitled to the land-rent of his estate only...

"If Ireland were in a sound and healthy state, and the people were well educated, the Irish landlord never would receive more than this land rent from his tenants. But, unfortunately, as agriculture forms the chief employment of the people, the possession of a farm is so much desired, that the competition amongst the tenants raises the sum paid to the landlord much above what he is entitled to" (p30).

"The tenant-right of Ulster when considered economically, is only a recognition, by long established custom, of the right of the tenant to the fair profit of the capital vested by him, by purchase of expenditure, in the permanent improvement of the land, or to the inherited profit arising from such improvements, when made by some of his ancestors." (p33.)

"It follows... that a tenant ought to receive, for tenant-right, such a sum as would be sufficient, if judiciously expended, to effect the improvements existing on the farm; and this sum may be called the natural price, or cost of production of tenant-right. The sum actually paid for tenant-right is often prevented from coinciding with this natural price, by disturbing causes, which it is necessary to notice. The disturbing causes I shall notice are three: indulgence of the landlords, excessive competition, and want of legal security" (35).

Tenant-right had its basis, and its economic justification, in particular production relations. The history of a particular peasantry before it became involved in those production relations will make it more or less capable of ensuring that its economic rights are not negated by the political force controlled by the landlords. The fact that the Ulster peasants had been involved in the Presbyterian struggles in Scotland made them particularly well fitted to look after their capitalist rights. On the other hand, the clan background and traditions of the Catholic peasantry would have hindered them in generating an independent movement for securing capitalist rights on the land. The fact that they had no history of independent democratic struggle against the aristocracy in the clan system undoubtedly facilitated the establishment of the rack-rent system in the 18th century. But eventually the new production relations in which they found themselves developed in them the power to struggle for the capitalist rights.

The Land League Struggles were not "kinship right... re-appear(ing) as capitalist right". The Land Leaguers were a product of the bourgeois world. They were not clansmen striving after the old world. They were farmers asserting their rights in the new bourgeois world that was developing in Southern Ireland, having freed themselves from 'kinship' notions.

The Imperialist View   The Presbyterian tenant-right leader of the 1840s, and a leader of the tenant-right "League of North and South" in the 1850s, James M'Knight, asked:

"What is the *value* of Irish landlordism to the State, that it should be maintained at the cost so enormous, and, if not seasonably terminated, at a cost eventually so ruinous to England?" (**The Ulster Tenant Right**, p56).

Tenant-right was a definite capitalist property right. Why should a capitalist state refuse to recognise it? Marx, writing in 1853, gave a very forceful answer to this question:

"'Nothing could tend', concludes The Times with regard to tenant-right, 'to greater confusion than such *communistic distribution of ownership*. The only person with any right in the land is the landlord'.

"The Times seems... never to have heard of the hot controversy going on... upon the claims of the landlord, not among social reformers and Communists, but among the very political economists of the British middle class. Ricardo, the creator of modern political economy in Britain, did not controvert the 'right' of the landlords, as he was quite convinced that their claims were based upon fact, not upon right, and that political economy in general had nothing to do with the question of right—but he attacked the land monopoly in a more unassuming, yet more scientific, and therefore more dangerous manner. He proved that the private proprietorship in land, as distinguished from the respective claims of the labourer, and of the farmer, was a relation quite superfluous in, and incoherent with, the whole framework of modern production; that the economical expression of that relationship and the rent of the land might, with great advantage be appropriated by the State, and finally that the interest of the landlord was opposed to the interest of all the other classes of modern society...

"Thus, from the very point of view of modern English political economists, it is not the usurping English landlord but the Irish tenants and labourers, who have the only right in the soil of their native country." **(The Indian Question—Irish Tenant Right**, June 28, 1853.)

The British industrial capitalist class soon justified the views of Marx and Ricardo on the nature of capitalist class interest with relation to landlordism by taking up the cause of the Irish tenants against the Irish landlords, and abolishing the latter as an effective social class.

Due to the fact of land monopoly (i.e., the fact that only a definite quantity of land exists), the evolution of property relations on the land is more complex than in industry. The British ruling class has always been cautious about changing land law. But when new property relations have actually evolved, making the law inadequate, they have always been prepared to bring the law into line with the reality.

In 1838, the Tipperary landlords asked Dublin Castle for a campaign of coercion against the Tipperary peasants, who were making a great deal of trouble for them. The reply of the Irish Under-Secretary, Thomas Drummond (which was made public through the House of Commons), was immediately adopted as the manifesto of the tenant movement. He wrote:

"Property has duties as well as rights; to the neglect of those duties in times past, is mainly to be ascribed that diseased state of society in which such crimes take their rise; and it is not in the enactment or enforcement of statutes of extraordinary severity, but chiefly in the better and more faithful performance of those duties, and the more enlightened and humane exercise of those rights, that a permanent remedy for such disorders is to be sought."

The Southern landlords, of course, did not and could not become more 'enlightened'. (In a degenerate land system 'enlightened' landlordism would only lead to bankruptcy.) But the state had issued a warning that its interests were not identical with the landlords' interests.

In 1869, during another period of agrarian disturbance, a book called **The Irish Land**, by George Campbell was published. Campbell was not a representative of the tenant, or the radical Liberal, movements. He was a representative of the governing section of the ruling class, being the Chief Commissioner of the Central Provinces of India. He wrote:

"In Ireland there are two sets of laws—the English laws, and the laws and customs of the country, which, enforced in a different way" [i.e., through agrarian outrage] "are as active and effective. In the clashing of these two systems lies the whole difficulty. In the assumption that the theoretical English law is the only law, and the attempt to put out of sight the customary law of the country, lies the fallacy of the argument on behalf of the landlords. In theory the landlords are absolute owners, but in fact are they so? Most assuredly not. The extreme theory of property is everywhere overborne and modified by custom. In the North that custom has assumed a definite and recognized form, against which it is vain for the landlords to contest. There is peace, but peace at the expense of the extreme theory of landlord property. In the South the custom is not so well settled; there is social and religious discord, the agitated waters have not admitted of the perfect crystallisation of that tenant-right element which still exists... By an infinitely more disagreeable process, a similar result is arrived at in the South as in the North... vis., that the theoretical landlord cannot do what he likes with what he considers to be his land... The landlord by the consent of both sides, is entitled to his rent, and he gets his rent without difficulty. But if he tries to take possession of the land as his own, or to give it to whom he chooses, he is at once met by a law stronger than the law—he cannot do it—; he has the rent, but he has not the land. The people have, in one sense, the land, but they have not the support of the law administered by the ordinary tribunals...

"Talk of the sacredness of landlord property as you will, it is quite impossible for anyone to hear the common language of, and read the literature regarding, Ireland, without feeling that, law or no law, at this moment the landlords are not the only owners of the soil. All classes talk freely, as a matter of course, of a man 'owning a farm', 'selling a farm' etc.... It is well-known that tenants habitually dispose of their farms by formal will" (p7).

"The tenant-right of the north is the right to sell the right of occupancy... the 'good-will' it is frequently called... for the value which it will fetch in the market. This represents the combined value of the privilege of occupancy and of the buildings and improvements of the tenant... The tenant-right is really a very beneficial co-proprietorship of the somewhat indefinite and uncertain character of rights held by custom rather than by law." (p46-7.)

"Many deny that there is tenant-right beyond Ulster—but the assertion when analysed means... that there is not the Ulster tenant-right nor any definite well established custom in the quasi-legal sense. On many estates and in particular parts of the country, the custom is almost as well established as in Ulster—in others, it is only as it were inchoate and rudimentary. But this I maintain, that wherever we have any trace of it, the practice takes the Ulster form. It may differ from the Ulster tenant-right as the sapling differs from the full grown oak, but it is still the same species." (p125.)

Campbell recommended the legalisation of the Ulster Custom, and was clearly of the opinion that a half share in the land was all that the landlords could hope for, or were entitled to. It was all that they actually had. They could lose this part ownership, but they could not regain full ownership.

Ulster Custom was legalised in 1870, and became the basis of the government's land policy for the whole of Ireland.

It is worth quoting Campbell on another aspect of the question:

"It is sometimes said to be extraordinary and unaccountable that farmers give for the tenant right of a farm a price as high as the fee-simple of the land would fetch" [i.e., they pay as much to become the tenant as it would cost to become the landlord of a farm] "but then it must be remembered that what is called the fee-simple is only the landlord-right burdened with the tenant-right of another who is practically co-proprietor. It is quite intelligible that a farmer should give £40 for a right of occupancy carrying the possession he desires, rather than pay the same sum for a superior landlord-right which gives no possession. If the two rights could be sold together they might fetch £80; but I believe that a great majority of farmers would in such a case rather give £80 for the tenant-right of twenty acres than the same sum for the absolute fee-simple of ten acres." (p49.)

Montgomery was of the opinion that the legalisation of the Ulster Custom, and the policy of extending it throughout the country, would not settle the land question in the South:

"There are many reasons why the introduction of Ulster Custom throughout Ireland by means of compulsory legislation could not be a success. As has been shown it is not sufficiently elaborated to fit any relation of landlord and tenant where at least a germ of sympathy does not exist; for while favourable to the tenant in times of prosperity, his apparent liability to, and the seeming exemption of the landlord from, loss when he land is depreciated in value, strains their relations to one another. In the case of Ulster too the extraneous means of acquiring wealth, independent of the soil, by manufacturing pursuits provides a more or less constant supply of purchasers for the land when it comes into the market; while in other parts of Ireland the complete dependence of the population upon agriculture, though increasing the demand for land, restricts the possibility of there being the necessary capital for its purchase in times of depression. Hence the tenant-right would either become merely of nominal value, or else the incoming tenant would take the holding burdened by a load of debt accumulated in raising the purchase-money of the tenant-right, and so would be in no position either to do justice to the land, or to give much likelihood of being a satisfactory rent-payer." (History Of Land Tenure, p122.)

And so it turned out. Differences of religion and nationality between landlord and tenant in the South made compromise between them impossible. Further to that, the traditional landlord class (dating from the late 17th century) began to break up in the 1840s. A century and half of rackrenting a helpless peasantry resulted in large numbers of the landlords being, not millionaires, but virtual bankrupts. The Famine brought matters to a head. The peasants starved and the landlords couldn't get in a lot of their rents:

"In 1849, an Encumbered Estates Act was passed, giving creditors a prompt remedy against embarrassed land-owners. In... six months... 13 millions worth had come under operation of the new law." (C.G. Duffy, The League Of North And South, p24.)

"Large numbers of landlords whose estates were hopelessly involved, and to whom the famine with the attendant failure of rent and increase of taxation had brought ruin, flocked to the (Encumbered Estates) Courts. By the end of 1858 there had been 8,300 conveyances... The class of landlord created by the purchases had not been very satisfactory. The purely business element which characterised the purchase of land from the Courts as a speculation, excludes any feeling of reciprocal obligations founded on a bond of personal acquaintance as distinguished from legal relations, and the 'new man' proved even more obnoxious to the Irish peasant than the landlord to whose faults he was accustomed." (Montgomery p112.)

Ulster tenant-right proved to be no solution in the South. When this became clear, the British Tory Government decided (in 1903) to abolish the landlord system by enabling the farmers to buy out the landlords. The period of joint ownership lasted only 30 years in the South, and was superseded by farmer-ownership. The Southern landed gentry, being socially useless, withered away rapidly over most of the country as a consequence of the Tory Land Acts.

Lecky's Lament The historian, Lecky, was one of the most enlightened products of the Anglo-Irish ascendancy. He was, in fact one of the most effective critics of the Ascendancy (see his History Of Ireland In The 18th Century). One of his objectives in exposing the rack-renting landlord aristocracy of the Ascendancy was to help it change itself into a socially useful aristocracy of the kind that existed in Britain; an aristocracy charging reasonable rents, superintending their estates, fostering improved methods of agriculture, and on this basis maintaining a place for themselves in the political life of capitalist society.

But the British ruling class, through both its Liberal and Tory representatives, gave up the Southern Irish landlords as a bad loss. Its assault on Irish landlordism from 1870 onwards shocked Lecky, and went against his whole conception of property rights.

In **Democracy & Liberty** (1899) Lecky complained that "the landlord has ceased to be an owner. He has become merely a rent-charger" (Volume 1, p186). Furthermore, he was not even allowed to charge a rent in accordance with market conditions. Rents were made subject to political arbitration.

The Act of 1870, which made Ulster Custom the basis of land law, did not give fixity of tenure to the tenant. Lecky quotes government speeches in the 1870 debate, which admitted that "perpetuity of tenure on the part of the occupier is virtually expropriation of the landlord". The landlords were assured that the government had no plans in mind for expropriating them. But that

"did not prevent the legislators of 1881 conferring fixity of tenure to the present tenant without granting compensation to the landlord, and from that time the first principle of much reasoning in Parliament about Irish land has been that it is dual ownership; and the landlord is nothing more than a partner, or, as it is now the fashion to say, 'a sleeping partner', in a joint possession, whose interests in every question of dispute should be systematically subordinated to those of the other partner... The Legislator has deprived the landlord of the plainest and most inseparable rights of ownership... the power of making contracts, offering his farms at the market price; selecting his tenants; prescribing the period and the time for which he will let his land. A court is established with an absolute power of deciding the amount of rent which the tenant is to pay, and the landlord has no option of refusing, or seeking another tenant" (p187).

"The Act of 1881 appears to me one of the most... extreme violations of the rights of property in the whole history of English legislation... Before the legislation of Mr. Gladstone the ownership of land in Ireland was, like that in France and America, as absolute and undisputed as the ownership of a house, or a horse, or a yacht". The Act of 1881 ended all of that. "It has been described by one of the best continental writers upon government (Laveleye) as an attack upon the principle of property more radical than any measure of the French Revolution, or even of the Reign of Terror." (p192.)

When a Liberal Government was eroding the legal right of landlords, the Unionist (Tory) Party opposed it, but when the Unionists were in government, they pressed ahead with the same kind of legislation for the tenants and against the landlords. Parliamentary assurances given to the landlords at each stage were completely disregarded a short while later, when the time was ripe for the next stage of the transfer of ownership. Nothing was allowed to stand in the way of the triumph of capitalist right on the land. It was not for nothing that Engels described the British Parliament as the most revolutionary institution of the 19th century.

Through these means the Southern landlords were so thoroughly demoralised that they were only too glad to co-operate in liquidating themselves when, a few years after Lecky wrote the above, a Unionist government proposed to bring the capitalist agrarian revolution to a conclusion by establishing the farmers in absolute ownership of the land. By this time, the only real issue was whether or not they would be compensated for their loss of ownership.

The agrarian revolution described here took place through class struggle. At particular moments, there were conflicts between the tenants' movement and the State. But the leaders of the tenants placed great reliance on their assumption that the British ruling class interest was basically sympathetic with the interest of the tenants. And such proved to be the case.

The Linen Trade

The Ulster tenant was not simply a farmer. In fact, Ulster farming was thought to be a disgrace to the profession by Arthur Young, a public spirited English farmer who toured Ireland in the 1770s:

"You there behold a province peopled by weavers; it is they who cultivate, or rather beggar the soil, as well as work the looms; agriculture there is in ruins... the whole region is a disgrace to the kingdom; all the crops you see are contemptible, are nothing but filth and weeds." (**Tour In Ireland**, Volume 2, p192.)

The tenant farmers became involved in the linen trade, and the growth of the linen trade prolonged the existence of small holdings. Conrad Gill describes this development as follows:

"The growth of the linen trade meant... not a growth of towns, except as marketing centres, but the spread of manufacture over the whole countryside..." (p31).

"The flax crop is a difficult, laborious and uncertain crop to grow, and at first glance it seems rather strange that peasants with minute holdings, and scarcely any capital, should care to risk their livelihood in such an enterprise... The explanation was, in the first place, that a flax crop yielded on the whole a larger return from a given area of land than any other crop which a peasant could grow; and secondly, that the careful hand-labour needed in its harvesting made it particularly suitable for very small holdings. Further, the preparation of yarn, although it was ill-paid labour, brought at any rate some increase to the trifling income of the clothier's household. In certain parts of the country flax crops were the more attractive because they were exempted by custom from tithes. Moreover, it was found that flax could be grown satisfactorily after potatoes... which were also exempted from tithes... and thus the small farmer who knew nothing of the Norfolk system could at least use a flax crop in establishing a simple rotation" (**The Rise Of The Irish Linen Industry** p35).

The Ulster small-holder, then, was a participant in an industry which spread throughout the countryside. The peculiarities of the linen industry (in which the technical development facilitating centralisation lagged far behind the cotton industry), combined with the particular form of land tenure in Ulster, resulted in a mixture of farming and handicrafts, which was very different from that prevailing under feudalism since it was petty bourgeois in character and depended on the demand of the modern capitalist market.

R.R. Kane, in his **Industrial Resources Of Ireland** (1844) remarked on the difference between flax growing and the growing of other crops:
"The great value of it to this country is… that its cultivation supplies not merely a source of agriculture, but also of manufacturing employment. In this respect it is far more beneficial than a food crop of the same money value, or occupying the same ground. The flax, as it leaves the land of the farmer, gives a livelihood to the dresser, from whom it passes to the spinner, to the weaver, to the bleacher, and perhaps the embroiderer." (p336.)

Kane's remarks on hemp production also apply in great part to flax:
"…the amelioration of the process of cultivation requires a very extended knowledge of chemical and mechanical science. That husbandry as an art, so far from presenting the monotonous and almost passive routine in which rustic existence has been dreamed away, requires to be placed parallel with the other great departments of human occupation, in the amount of intelligence which its successful practice calls into play." (p343.)

The development of the linen trade in Ulster in the 18th century created a mass petty bourgeois basis for the development of capitalism, and in the course of the 19th century large scale industry arose on this basis. Catholic nationalist propagandists usually argue that the fact that a flourishing linen trade developed only in Ulster was due to the schemes of the British government. It "allowed" the linen trade to develop in Ulster in accordance with the policy of "divide and rule". And it "allowed" industrial capitalism to develop in Ulster in the 19th century for the same reason. These views have nothing in common with the actual course of history in Ireland. Furthermore, they are absurd in principle, since they assume that capitalism can be created by government administration. A vigorous capitalist development, such as that which occurred in Ulster in the 18th/19th centuries, could not possibly have resulted from bureaucratic schemes.

It is sometimes asserted that the linen trade was created by the policies of Thomas Wentworth, the Earl of Strafford, who was the Irish Viceroy in the 1630s. Strafford was a renegade from the Parliamentary party in England, who went over to the monarchy and became its ablest politician. The power of the absolute monarchy was coming under increasing pressure from the Parliamentary forces in England, and Strafford conceived the scheme of establishing a strong counter-revolutionary base for the King in Ireland. He raised a large Catholic army for use against Parliament, and made efforts to develop a linen industry as a source of revenue for the Crown. His policies had some short term result of a superficial kind, but historically had only a marginal effect.

Another view is that the trade resulted from the Huguenot immigration of the late 17th and early 18th centuries. For example: "At first the industry was not confined to Ulster, but, as time went on, that province, owing mainly, it would seem to the impetus administered by Crommelin, came to engross the manufacture" (D.A. Chart, **Economic History**, p68). This view has somewhat more substance than the last. The Huguenots were French Protestants who fled from persecution in France. They were experienced in the most modern methods of linen manufacture and undoubtedly had a beneficial effect on the trade in Ireland. However, though large numbers of them settled in Ulster (Lisburn being a largely Huguenot town by origin), they also settled in large numbers in the South, particularly in Cork. But they had no great success in developing the trade in the South. They helped the economic development of Ulster because Ulster was developing economically anyhow.

Louis Crommelin, one of the Huguenot leaders, was made "Overseer of the Royal Linen Manufacture of the Kingdom", and in 1705 published **An Essay Towards The Improving Of The Hempen And Flaxen Manufacture In Ireland**. He observed:

"As to the soil of this country, all the Kingdom (*except from Dundalk northwards*) will bear as good Hemp as the World affords—nay, I may say better…" (p4, our emphasis).

His essay is a practical handbook on the manufacture of linen. He said: "there is not one part of the Linen Manufacture wherein I am not able to work with my own hands." But Robert Stephenson, a linen manufacturer who reviewed the trade in the 1750s, was very critical of Crommelin's practical knowledge of the trade, and of his lack of adaptation to Irish conditions. According to Stephenson:

"…his last chapter contains his whole theory and practical knowledge of Bleaching, and by following the Directions he lays down in his Course of Operation, I will venture to say it is impossible to make a white Piece of Linen; his scheme is the most expensive I have ever met with… nor indeed do I believe he ever made a high white Piece of Linen or had any Knowledge of this Part of the Mystery (as he terms it)…" (All quotations are from the collection of Stephenson's Reports published in 1757, under the title: **Inquiry Into The State And Progress Of Linen Manufacture**.)

Stephenson was also critical of the general influence of the Huguenots on economic policy. He alleged that "the French Managers meant to create a Monopoly in their favour," for example, by introducing long apprenticeships from which they were exempt.

The trade was placed under the control of a Linen Board, which had large sums at its disposal for subsidy. It was far from being the case that disproportionate subsidies were given to Ulster. The contrary was the case. The Board did not see the merits of the sprawling peasant industry in the North, and looked much more favourably on the more fashionably organised manufacturers in the South. And the relative developments in North and South show, in every case, that a powerful industry cannot be subsidised into existence.

Linen Board expenditure in the four provinces between 1737 and 1757 (as cited by Gill, p101), was as follows:

Leinster	£ 156,338
Munster	59,440
Connaught	49,477
Ulster	40,380

Stephenson, a private manufacturer with a sense of public duty to his class, was highly critical of the Linen Board, and was concerned about the intelligent use of subsidies. It was the business of the Board to know the particulars of the Linen Trade in general, and the particular circumstances in each county, and to guide the trade, directing each county into the branch of the trade best suited to it, taking market demand into account, and stimulating each county "by a small and well regulated Premium for that County, …lead the Inhabitants in that Branch which shall appear most suitable to the Nature of their Yarn and Spinning". However, as it was, there was no flexibility in the trade, no intelligent response to the market. Bad linen was produced because natural variations from county to county were not taken into account. Particular kinds of linen were produced, not primarily because they were suitable to the environment or were in demand, but because it was generally known how to produce them, and for the same reason commodities which were in demand were not produced.

These were the problems accompanying the introduction of the industry in the form of capitalism from above, in a society where the mass basis for capitalist production had not developed. A Linen Board of exceptional technical and commercial ability and a strong sense of public duty were required to compensate for the general backwardness of the economy. But the general backwardness of the economy made it impossible to have such a Board.

But in Ulster the trade looked after itself. According to Stephenson,

"...the Disparity between the manufacturers of the *North* and *South* of the same Species or Denominations of Linen is frequently so great, that it is impossible to vend them either at Home or Abroad for the same Uses" (p18). "Manufacturers in the Southern Provinces generally meet with the most discouraging Circumstances in their Efforts to vie with the Province of Ulster in the few Branches the People of the *North* by unwearied Application became the master of" (p17).

"It will appear that our Natives unassisted by the Linen-Board, have struck out Branches entirely new, which they have carried to such Degrees of perfection, by their Ingenuity and Industry, as to have gained them Reputations abroad, tho' neglected at home" (p63). "It is thought necessary to advertise the Publick that altho' the Advantages this country derives are generally ascribed (by Strangers) to the prudent Distribution of the Linen Fund, yet it will appear that Necessity arising from our confined Circumstances with respect to Trade, and the Ingenuity of our Inhabitants, have a much greater share therein" (p67).

"In the Province of Ulster, while the Linen Manufacture has become of such Consequence, as to counter-ballance all the Luxuries imported into the Kingdom, it is conducted in the most convenient and easy Method that can be prescribed, so as to promote industry and avoid Disputes: there the Draper, Weaver and Spinner meet in publick Market; the Draper to buy such Linens as suit his Purpose; the Weaver to dispose of such Linen as he hath made of the Yarn bought in Market, and the Spinner to dispose of her Yarn, and buy Flax; by this means all are independent of each other, and only expect to be paid according to their Merits.

"In order to promote the same scheme as much as possible throughout the Kingdom, I would recommend giving £100 Premium in manner following, in twenty five Counties, and drop them as Markets become considerable in each County... (except the Counties of Antrim, Down, Derry, Tyrone, Armagh, Monaghan and Cavan; those have good Markets and no occasion for this Premium) to the Merchant or Draper who should buy and export on his account..." (p203).

It will be seen that the seven counties which Stephenson (170 years before Partition) excluded from his subsidy scheme, on the grounds that their market development made subsidy unnecessary, includes five of the six counties of Northern Ireland, the other two being Border counties.

In the North production was overwhelmingly petty bourgeois, and the mass of the people were involved in marketing their own products. Capitalist centralisation grew slowly, consolidating itself with each advance. In the South production was artificially centralised and capitalised. This introduction, from outside and from above, of capitalist production into a society of rackrenting landlords and rack-rented peasants, created numerous problems, technical, commercial and social. The industry was highly vulnerable to market fluctuation, had little or no internal power of technological change, and was riddled with labour troubles. These causes led to the breakdown of the industry in the South, while it continued to develop in the North, and thus the uneven development of the market, which was already significant in 1750, was considerably aggravated.

The Development Of The Linen Industry Gill describes the organisation of the Ulster linen industry in the early 18th century as follows:

"The method of securing raw material tended strongly in itself to keep the linen manufacture both rustic and simply organised. A certain proportion of the raw flax—and in the early days a great proportion—was grown at home by the weaver himself: consequently he was not dependant on a merchant for his supplies. The webs that he produced were his own property, and in his dealings with the market he was a trader as well as a craftsman" (p33). "It was impossible for each weaver to grow exactly the quality and quantity of flax that he needed for his own loom. On the other hand many farmers had more flax than they needed, especially those in the southern provinces, or the non-manufacturing districts of Ulster. Thus there was scope for traffic in flax between growers and weavers. The trade was carried on, no doubt, by the class of jobbers who also brought yarn to the manufacturing centres; and it led to the growth of flax markets over the whole of Ulster, some in the chief towns, for sale to the weavers, others in small, remote towns and villages, for collection from the growers. As a rule, however, the growers would prefer to sell their flax in the form of yarn, in order that their womenfolk might gain the price of spinning" (p38).

"The jobber obtained his yarn in various ways, sometimes buying it at fairs, sometimes collecting it from door to door, or even, for convenience, receiving it at church. He would in any case pay cash to the spinner. He would then carry the yarn... to the linen markets of Ulster, and there dispose of it to weavers—or later to drapers and manufacturers. The jobbers business led to the organisation of yarn markets... When these markets were established is not clear, but the jobbers were certainly at work in 1727" (p39).

"At first, when a web was finished (i.e. by the weaver), it was sold in a fair; but as trade increased it became worth while to hold weekly or fortnightly markets for brown or unbleached cloths... The sellers were weavers, who attended each market in large numbers to dispose of cloth woven by themselves... The buyers were middlemen, known as drapers, who were fewer in number" (p42-3).

"Although the weavers were for so long independent or semi-independent dealers, it was not intended by the government or by the early projecters of the industry that they should remain so. The ruling authorities clearly had in view a large-scale capitalistic organisation. In the first regulating statute of 1705, it was provided that weavers should be freemen of their boroughs, and in 1709 an apprenticeship of five years was prescribed before the weaver could become a master craftsman. These clauses assumed that the industry would be carried on by urban workers, who could be controlled by a class of employing merchants—especially by the Huguenots, who inspired much of the legislation of this period. Moreover, the numerous schemes for exploiting the linen trade which were begun, and in most cases ended, between 1690 and 1700, all contemplated an industry centred in towns and organised on a large scale by means of joint-stock... But as a contemporary observer wisely said, 'I have seen frequent attempts of this nature come to very little'... Industry avoided the towns, and the weaver retained his independence.

"He was in a very real sense the mainstay of the industry... Time after time attempts were made in all parts of the country to set up manufacture on capitalistic lines, and nearly always the attempts failed within a few years. It was the independent farmers of Ulster who formed the basis of success" (p43-4).

It was only in the production of cambric and damask (luxury products) that effective centralisation took place in this early period.

"The small capital of a thrifty peasant could be used in acquiring a loom, building a weaving shed, or buying raw material. The profits of manufacture in turn could be invested in land, or in hiring additional workers. By such means a peasant could become in a few years' time both a substantial farmer and a substantial manufacturer. A great proportion of the employing class which appeared later in the linen trade seem actually to have raised their fortunes in this way" (p48).

"When the farmer had woven his cloth he generally disposed of it in the brown, unfinished state. The bleaching and finishing processes were managed by men of greater substance. Before the 18th century, when linen was chiefly made for use at home, the cloth was often bleached by the farmer's wife... But the method was slow, primitive, inefficient, and when a really good finish was desired the web was usually sent to Holland to be bleached at Haarlem... Near to the beginning of the 18th century, however, and perhaps earlier, specialized bleachers appeared in Ireland to meet the needs of the expanding trade. Many of them were probably Huguenots... There is evidence that a fair number of bleachworks had been set up by the year 1725... Without doubt many other bleachgreens were opened in the second quarter of the century, and bleaching became a very important branch of the industry. It was not only that the greater volume of trade made specialised bleaching a paying concern. There was the further reason that in this period some of the more advanced and delicate kinds of manufacture were developing—the fine yard-wides of south Antrim, the cambric, lawn, diaper, and damask of Armagh and south Down—which demanded a high degree of skill in bleaching and finishing. Even then the processes were by no means efficient, and bleachgreens were as a rule quite small concerns... It was not until the last decade of the century that bleaching attained to a really large scale, or made any approach to scientific method. Nevertheless, by 1725 it had already passed beyond the reach of the ordinary weaver.

"Not only were weavers no longer able to bleach on their own account: in most cases they could not even afford to deal with bleachers... Thus, as a result of the more advanced methods of bleaching, there arose a class of middlemen known as drapers. The normal business of the draper was to buy brown linen for cash from weavers; to contract for the bleaching and finishing... then, several months later, to dispose of the white cloth, usually to merchants and exporters in Dublin.

"There is no definite evidence of the origin of the drapers' class or the date of their appearance... We may safely assume that drapers were becoming a distinct class about 1720, at the time when specialised bleaching was developing, for the presence of bleachers implied the existence of drapers. In all probability many of the early drapers were shopkeepers who had made a practice of buying linen at fairs. They would keep part of the stock in their shops, and would sell some brown linen to larger merchants, who would export it to Holland for finishing. Their ordinary business would supply them with capital, and would enable them to build up a connexion from small beginnings as the linen trade increased. The Drapers had their heyday between 1740 and 1780. In the last few years of the century their position began to be assailed by wealthy merchants, who used more advanced methods, and could give longer credit" (p51-2).

"An important change in organisation connected with the rise of drapers was the substitution of brown linen markets for fairs... When markets were well established, special halls were built in certain towns, chiefly in the most important centres of trade, such as Belfast, Londonderry, Ballymena, Banbridge, and Lisburn... Since the manufacture by 1750 was spread over a great part of Antrim, Down, Armagh, Londonderry, and Tyrone, there must have been some dozens of markets to meet the requirements of weavers.

"For about a century—roughly from 1730 to 1830—brown linen markets were one of the leading characteristics of the industry in Ulster. It was not so in the southern provinces. We have seen that the system of land tenure there did not lend itself to abundant markets and fairs for agricultural produce. Neither did the capitalistic methods of manufacture, which were common in the south, favour the growth of markets. There were, I believe, more than two dozen such markets, and most of them very small. The only one which really flourished was at Drogheda, and that market was of a peculiar type, supplied by manufacturing employers in place of small weavers... But seeing that Ulster soon gained a great preponderance in manufacture, it is true to say that most of the Irish linen trade in the period we have been describing (1725-50) passed through local markets, and was organised by the three classes of farmer-weavers, drapers and bleacher" (p52-5).

But there was an increasing overlap between the bleachers and drapers, many drapers going in for bleaching, and many bleachers procuring their own supply of brown linen for bleaching and sale by themselves, in addition to that which they bleached for drapers.

"The chief interest in the industrial history of Ulster after 1750 is the growth of new groups of producers and new social relationships... A rapid extension of trade almost necessarily brings important changes in organisation, and these changes in turn react on the social position and functions of the various classes of producers. The development often takes place so quietly that it leaves little trace in history, until some striking event suddenly reveals the forces that have been remoulding society. The 'turn out' of 1782, and the battle of pamphlets which followed, serves this purpose in the history of Ulster. They show the old system of domestic manufacture and sale in open markets was gradually yielding to new methods, and that a drift towards capitalism had begun. This disclosure would be surprising if we had no source of information other than official documents..." (p138).

Gill then describes the "Rising of 1762". This event is unknown to those 'socialist' hangers-on of Catholic nationalism, for whom the only real things that happen in Ireland are those which happen in Catholic Ireland. It was left to a scientific bourgeois economic historian to investigate the first major political conflict caused by the development of capitalism in Ireland. The immediate occasion of the outbreak was trivial: a bill relating to the inspection of brown

linen—
"the three classes of journeymen, independent weavers, and small manufacturers were united at the beginning of the crisis of 1762, in opposition to the system of sealing brown linens. The fact is that there was a twofold purpose in the rising. In the first place, the weavers and small manufacturers who sold in the markets wished to work in their own way without being subject to inspection, which, as they feared, might be used in the interests of the drapers... From this point of view the 'turn out' of 1762 was only one event in the age-long rivalry between commercial and industrial capital. This aspect of it soon passed since the weavers and manufacturers found they had nothing to fear from the new system of inspection.

"But, in the second place, the journeymen had joined in the contest with the object of securing a standard wage and the right to combine... Bleachers... not only employed bleachyard workers and weavers, but were usually the buyers up of brown linen in addition; so that every class concerned in the rising had a grievance against them. But the manufacturers were soon appeased. Their alliance with the journeymen broke down; and in all probability the friendship of the former allies cooled very fast, for the manufacturers as employers of labour, would have little liking for the journeymen's programme. The invitation to the first mass meeting at Dromore in 1762 was addressed to "all gentlemen manufacturers and weavers"; but manufacturers were excluded from the mass meeting at Hillsborough in 1763, unless they themselves worked at the loom. The rift between capital and labour was in fact deeper and more lasting than the misunderstanding between buyers and sellers in the market" (p147-8).

"There was evidently in 1762 a fairly large class of permanent employees in Ulster. They were already strong enough, and class conscious enough, to organise a series of meetings, to carry out a formidable strike, and state their case with considerable ability in the public press" (142).

Though the great majority of the weavers still remained independent, the point of growth was in the classes of employers and wage workers. According to Gill:

"The number of weavers in Ulster appears... to have been about 35,000 in 1770 and 40,000 in 1784. Their division into independent craftsmen and wage-earners can only be roughly guessed... We may conclude that in 1770 about 35% of the weavers were employed by large or small manufacturers, and in 1784, rather more than 40% (p162).

About 1780 there was a spectacular development of capitalist factory production in Ulster which transformed Belfast into a manufacturing city. But it occurred in cotton production. It was not until the 1820s that the factory production of linen got going, coinciding with the decline of cotton production. In this period, the advancement of technique in linen production prepared the industry for factory production. The factory system created by the cotton industry was therefore able to change over to linen in the late 1820s.

Gill describes the organisation of the linen industry in 1820 as follows. It

"could be classified into three nearly equal groups, the first consisting of cloth made by small craftsmen and sold in the market, the second of cloth made for small manufacturers and sold by them in the market, the third made for larger employers and sold privately, or made for the bleachers by direct employment. The classification is clearer since each of these methods of production was typical of particular parts of Ulster" (p272).

The third category (large employers) was characteristic of the bleaching districts:

"we may mark out the east of Londonderry, the south of Antrim, the centre and west of Down, and the north of Armagh, as districts where capitalism was the most fully developed." (p273.)

"There was a sharp contrast to all of this change and activity in the simple and stable organisation of some other areas, notably north Antrim, Tyrone, parts of Londonderry, and the outlying districts in general. In these places trade was still in the hands of independent weavers, drapers and jobbers" (p274.)

"Near the southern boundary of Ulster, in south Armagh and north Monaghan, there was a peculiar system not found elsewhere to anything like the same extent... Nearly all the coarse linens produced in this district were made in the south of Armagh and the north of Monaghan, and a great proportion of the coarse cloth sold in the market at Armagh. A working weaver could not easily travel so far to market, and in all probability a good deal of flax from the southern provinces and from the Baltic States was used. On both these grounds there was an economic gain in marketing by small manufacturers; but the manufacturer had not yet such facilities for credit and accumulation of capital that he could develop trade on a large scale, and deal directly with exporters, or export on his own account. Therefore his sales were still made for cash to drapers or linen buyers in the open market; and as the market of Armagh was one of the largest in Ulster, there must have been a numerous body of manufacturers dealing there" (p275).

(It is important to bear this economic structure of Ulster in mind when considering political development after the 1780s. The political history of Ulster from the 1780s to the 1820s—including the history of the Orange Order—is something which remains to be written. All that has been written since the late 19th century, especially on the Nationalist side, is a projection backwards of contemporary propaganda. The writers have shown little or no acquaintance with the economic situation in which those political developments—particularly the Orange/Defender conflict—took place.)

In the late 1820s machine spinning was developed:

"In 1829 John Mulholland, who had been a cotton spinner and a user of steam power, set up a mill in York Street, Belfast. His cotton mill had been burnt down, and he decided to turn to the linen trade and try the experiment of applying the new motive power to the new wet-spinning machinery... The success of Mulholland's enterprise gave a still further impulse to the use of spinning machinery. Mills, independent of a head of water, could be set up on any convenient site... Consequently the number of mills soon increased. There were forty in Ireland in 1838; by 1853 the number had grown to 80: (p318).

Who Was 'Favoured'? To assess the extent to which the development of the industry in Ulster resulted in special treatment for Ulster, we will consider a number of ways this might have occurred: special legislation, disproportionate subsidies, large inflow of external capital, availability of large scale marketing facilities, availability of credit facilities.

There was no special legislation. What legislation there was was designed to favour the southern organisation of the trade, and was unfavourable to Ulster. The linen industry, like the land custom, of Ulster developed without the help of the law, and often against the law. Gill remarks: "While Parliament was passing... inoperative laws the linen trade was growing rapidly on its own account".

As to grants and subsidies, these went overwhelmingly to the South. Established marketing centres, and availability of merchant's capital also favoured the South, as did the inflow of capital in the 18th century. So did the established credit and banking facilities.

The Bank of Ireland in Dublin, founded in 1783, was given a monopoly of joint-stock banking until 1824. As to private banking, it was legally reserved to the gentry. Nobody who was engaged in industry or commerce would be granted a license to set up a private bank. Banking was therefore closed to the people who were best fitted to engage in it.

"Inexperienced landlords and adventurous rent-agents could still become bankers... Failures of banks were especially common during the next half-century [i.e., after 1755 when the law was passed]... While incompetent or unprincipled men were not debarred from setting up banks, responsible tradesmen were prohibited. Now it was men of this type—the Barclays, Lloyds, Dales, Smiths, and Barings—who were the pioneers of banking in Scotland and England. They were traders or manufacturers who adopted banking in the first instance as a secondary branch of business. By their services to their own country we can judge the disservice to Ireland of this restrictive act" (Gill, p169).

"If there had been county banks of the English type in Ulster, the small manufacturer could have increased the scale of his business, and could have dealt directly with Dublin, England and foreign countries, giving credit on his own account. But since manufacturers had to rely for capital on their own savings, their businesses grew slowly and never grew far" (p172). "The want of credit... kept the manufacturing districts for a long time dependant on the Dublin market", and on Dublin merchants. (p170.)

In 1804, the only bank in Ulster was in Derry. When banking was freed in 1824, the banking system in Belfast sprang into being.

In the 18th century all roads led to Dublin, both physically and figuratively, and everything that was established and conservative tended to maintain that state of affairs. In the early 19th century, through the sheer economic development of the North-East, a system of communications centring on Belfast came into being.

The Sinn Fein View When a bourgeois nationalist movement developed in the South in the late 19th century, and found its ambition to rule the whole of Ireland thwarted by the large scale industrial development of Ulster, the movement felt obliged to deny that the development of Ulster owed anything in particular to the people of Ulster. This was partially to provide a moral justification for subjugating Ulster to Home Rule or Sinn Fein government. But there is no doubt that it was also partially due to a psychological need to attribute the development of Ulster to something other than the activity of its inhabitants. The Southern bourgeoisie was given an inferiority complex by industrial Ulster. To relieve this, it was necessary to attribute the development of Ulster to external causes. (This sense of industrial inferiority relieved by fantasy, combined with an enormous sense of moral superiority, is a significant element in the bourgeois national culture of the Catholic community. It is unfortunate that it has been carried over to a great extent into the working class movement.)

Arthur Griffith wrote that, when England legislated against the Irish woollen industry in the 1690s, she

"declared she would encourage the linen industry. This she did not do...

To save the industry the Irish Parliament used the money of the country at large to sustain the linen manufacturers of the North. The process continued for many years until they were able to stand on their own legs, and defy English competition. The shipbuilding industry of Belfast owed its importance to a German, who supplied the capital and the ability on which it has arisen. On these two industries, one built up through a hundred years by the Irish Parliament, and the other built up by a German, Belfast subsists industrially. No serious effort is made to develop in any other direction. A great alkali industry was started, but it was let drop. Sitting on the edge of a great coalfield, Belfast makes no effort to raise its own coal, but remains sluggishly dependent on Scotland for the supply of an imperative essential of its existence." (**Nationality**, 2 August, 1919. See also, 17 February, 1917.)

Thus, in his bureaucratic fantasies, the representative of a weak but aspiring industrial capitalism made himself feel industrially superior to the large scale industrial capitalists of the North. The industrial development of Ulster may be attributed to any absurd cause so long as it is an external cause, but it may not be attributed to the causes which actually brought it about, because they were native to Ulster.

Appendix

Cotton With regard to the cotton industry: that too met with more official favour in the South, where it began earlier, was organised more lavishly and was very unsuccessful. In Ulster it was established by vigorous capitalist enterprise—especially by the families of Joy, McCabe and McCracken who were in the vanguard of the Volunteer and United Irish developments. They saw an opportunity, learned from scratch how to manufacture cotton by going to England to observe the process, and then set up highly successful enterprises in Belfast.

Wool & Linen George O'Brien, the chief economic historian of the Catholic nationalist school, makes some noteworthy comments on the linen industry. In his history of the 18th century he writes:

"The linen industry was of old standing in Ireland. As early as 1430 linen cloth was imported into England from Ireland... In the 16th century Spenser mentions that all Irishmen wore shirts made of linen, while the women wore linen turbans... When Strafford came to Ireland he conceived the idea of extending the linen industry" (**The Economic History Of Ireland In The 18th Century**, 1918, p189).

In his book on the 17th century he writes:

"until the Elizabethan war on Irish trade, the linen industry in Ireland occupied at least as important a place and was as fully developed as the woollen industry. The fiction that Ulster owes its great prosperity to Wentworth, who laid the foundation of a great linen industry to compensate Ireland for the woollen industry, which he proposed to discourage, is a convenient one for English historians who wish to present in as favourable a light as possible the less justifiable measures of English policy in Irish affairs. (**The Economic History Of Ireland In The 17th Century**, 1919, p76).

He gives a quote from Alice Stopford Green saying that linen was exported "in enormous quantities to foreign nations" (p76).

This is all said in the context of painting a long industrial history for Ireland. But, in another part of the same book, he writes:

"the encouragement of the linen industry was not an adequate compensation for the destruction of the woollen industry. The latter was a manufacture particularly suitable to Ireland; raw material was produced in Ireland in great quantities and of excellent quality; the foundation of its success had been laid by the labour and enterprise of many years. The linen industry, on the other hand, was concerned in working up a material which had never been grown as successfully as elsewhere: it had attained to whatever position it held by reason of much artificial encouragement and support; and as we know, it ultimately failed to spread to more than a small part of Ireland" (p230).

Comment on the obvious self-contradiction is unnecessary. The statement that wool was a great Irish industry should be understood in the spirit in which it was made, i.e., it is a useful statement to make in a particular argument. Two hundred pages earlier, in another context, it was useful to declare linen to have been a great Irish industry.

Wool According to William Petty (one of the founders of the science of political economy) in his **Political Anatomy Of Ireland** (1672) there were 4 million sheep in Ireland. "The Wool which is usually exported... grows upon 1,000,000 Sheep". The other three million provided for home consumption. But home consumption was only to a minor extent supplied through the market. An indication of the prevalence of subsistence production (which Petty reckoned to provide four-fifths of the needs of a peasant family), and the underdeveloped state (by comparison with Britain) of the home market, can be gathered from the following description by Petty:

"If it be true, that there are about 16,000 Families in Ireland, who have above one Chimney in their Houses; and above 180,000 others; It will be easily understood what the Trade of this latter sort can be, who use few Commodities; and thus such as almost everyone can make and produce. That is to say, Men live in such Cottages as they themselves can make in 3 or 4 Days; Eat such food (Tobacco excepted) as they buy not from others; wear such Cloaths as the Wooll of their own Sheep, spun into yarn by themselves doth make".

That is sufficient to show the absurdity of George O'Brien's statement that, in the 1690s, Ireland and England "had reached almost the same state of industrial development" (Economic History Of 17th Century, p225).

Woollen manufacture for the market was carried out by 30,000 "workers of wool and their wives". These were chiefly immigrant clothiers and wool-workers attracted by government policy. By 1798, the number had grown to 42,000 "Protestant families", with marginal Catholic involvement. In 1675, a manufacturer had written, "the whole quantity of what we work up in Ireland amounts to not half of what any one clothing county in England works up" (**Commercial Relations Between England And Ireland**, by A.E. Murray, 1903, quoted on p100).

Demand in Ireland for the cheaper kinds of cloth was low, since the peasantry produced their own. The market was chiefly for better quality cloth, and the production of this was poor both in quality and efficiency. Despite high duties against it, English cloth was imported in large quantities. When the export of woollen manufactures was banned in 1699, and there was a strong stimulus for Irish manufacturers to capture the Irish home market for the higher quality cloth, the industry failed to respond adequately to this stimulus, and extensive importation continued. There was a short lived fall in drapery imports from Britain, but they quickly picked up again.

The export of raw wool and woollen yarn to England was not banned. The export of woollen yarn (thread) rose considerably at this time:

1697—3,678 stones; 1700—26,617 stones; 1729—91,854 stones.

Another factor is that there was a vast increase in smuggling, estimated at

100,000 stones per annum. Nationalist historians who investigate the effects of legislation on trade merely quote the laws that were passed, and assume that they were enforced. But it would be more realistic to assume a very high level of inefficiency in the application of legislation that went against any reasonably vigorous economic tendency. The state machine was not then what it is now, especially in Ireland. And even in very recent times there have been extensive smuggling markets in Ireland. If the Irish woollen industry had been near the same stage of development as the English (which O'Brien alleges), it would certainly not have been squashed by legislation. If the legislation was very effective, it was only because the industry was to a great extent a creation of government policy, and in itself was very weak.

Since the ending of the protectionist era in the South (about 1960), a school of bourgeois economic historians has developed which is free to deal with this aspect of history in a factual way. The most eminent of these, L.M. Cullen, writes in his latest book:

"It is hard to see how the Irish woollen industry could have increased its exports significantly in the 18th century, or how the industry could have acquired a potential for transforming the Irish economy. The act of 1699 emerges as irrelevant in the main to the central problems of the first decade of the 18th century". (**Economic History Of Ireland Since 1600**, 1972, p42.)

In England, the woollen industry had developed first as an industry of small commodity producers, and was later central to the development of capitalist industry. That is to say, it played much the same part as linen did in Ulster. It was possible for small commodity production in wool to develop extensively in England in the 15th/16th century because the small producers could graze large numbers of sheep on the common lands which survived the feudal era. It is hard to see how an extensive small commodity woollen industry could have developed in Ireland. Extensive woollen manufacture would seem to imply ranching in Ireland: and the cry, *'Sheep replace men'*.

4. Grattan's Parliament

"One class of persons have been accustomed to look exclusively to Legislative interference for a removal of the evils to which Ireland is exposed; whilst others despair entirely of any beneficial effect upon her social condition from such interference. We do not agree with either of these classes. We know that the best directed measures of Parliament cannot produce the desired effect, unless aided and enforced by the steady, as well as active exertions of the people of all ranks and conditions in their respective spheres; but we are at the same time satisfied that a very beneficial change may be effected by the united and vigorous efforts of the Legislature, and of individuals"

(Report Of Devon Commission On The Occupation Of Land In Ireland, 1845).

Modern bourgeois Catholic Ireland draws its ideological forms chiefly from two sources: Catholicism and Gaelic Ireland. It is governed by a "Taoiseach", and his deputy is a "Tanaiste". Forms derived from Gaelic Ireland are to be found everywhere. But the actual values of the society are bourgeois. Gaelic Ireland judged itself by its own standards. It had its own vices and virtues. They were not the vices and virtues of capitalism. Gaelic Ireland, therefore, had no sense of inferiority with relation to England or to Anglo-Ireland. The O'Neill could pay a state visit to Tudor England in the 16th century, with the trappings and entourage of a Gaelic chief, and not feel morally intimidated. He was immune to Tudor social standards. Tudor England might view him as a barbarian. But, if he was a barbarian, he had barbarian moral standards. He was not a barbarian who was demoralised through being impregnated by the standards of civilisation.

But Catholic bourgeois Ireland is not convinced of its own official values, and does not judge itself by those values. It imposes Catholicism on the masses, it inculcates Catholic morality through the state, it imposes a Gaelic gloss on the society, but its actual standards are neither Catholic, nor Gaelic. Propagandists arise who advocate that either Catholic or Gaelic standards should be consistently applied in historical judgement and in contemporary social life. But these propagandists, instead of being pioneers or prophets, are merely the honoured eccentrics, the holy fools, of modern Catholic Ireland:— Because modern Catholic Ireland is thoroughly impregnated with a system of values which is in contradiction with its official values: it is thoroughly impregnated with capitalist values in their classical British form.

The Ulster barbarian chieftain of the 16th century had a profound conviction that he was the social equal of Elizabeth the First, regardless of the economic and cultural gulf between the two societies. In fact, he saw Elizabeth in terms of the clan system. Just as the 19th century bourgeois could only understand the hunting spear of an African savage as a miniature form of capital, the O'Neill could only understand Elizabeth as a great chief.

But the modern Catholic bourgeois, for all his Gaelic/Catholic ideology, judges the world by the standards that were made universal by British capitalism. The official ideology is for bamboozling the masses. The official ideology does not determine how the bourgeois sees himself with relation to Britain, or views the history of his own class. By comparison with the barbarian Gaelic chiefs, he is a demoralised person. So demoralised is he that, while affecting in the present a moral superiority with relation to Britain, he even applies British bourgeois standards when describing the Gaelic Ireland of the past, where such standards have no relevance. This was the case even with a serious antiquarian like Eoin MacNeill. It is carried into absurdity by T.P. Coogan, editor of the Irish Press, and the most influential bourgeois propagandist in Catholic Ireland: in his book, **Ireland Since The Rising**, he condemns the clans for not having the "commonsense" of the bourgeoisie.

The demoralisation resulting from this double standard has reduced Nationalist history to whining misrepresentation. It can apply neither the Gaelic world outlook, nor the Catholic (i.e., feudal) world outlook, nor the bourgeois world outlook consistently in interpreting Irish history. Catholic Ireland, in its bourgeois development, is hypersensitive to the standards of Protestant Britain. It falls well short of glory by these standards. But the reason it falls short must be represented as an entirely external reason.

The Irish Nationalist school of history might be called the *legislative* school of history. It sees the course of Irish history as being determined by British legislation. It does not even rise to the level of being a *bureaucratic* school of history. Legislation, even when there is no executive power of enforcing it, is all powerful. The real world is made up of Acts of Parliament.

The legislative view of history reaches its climax in Grattan's Parliament—in the Parliament itself, as well as in subsequent Nationalist views of it. The Parliament lacked an Executive arm. It merely legislated. Britain controlled the Executive. Grattan himself never troubled about vulgar bureaucratic matters. He made Parliamentary speeches and proposed motions, and expected actual social changes to follow from these words.

The great Westminster Parliamentarians were his inspiration, but the Parliament named after him was a parody of the Westminster Parliament. The British Parliament desired, and achieved, the substance of political power. It was not content to make speeches and pass motions. It wanted control over executive political power (the army, judiciary and civil service), and it fought a civil war to achieve this power. But Grattan's Parliament was a parliament without executive power.

The belief in the omnipotence of legislation is well brought in the following:
"What is known as Ulster tenant-right is supposed to have begun when the province was 'planted' in the time of James I... That right was not founded on law, but on custom. Any landlord who chose might disregard it." M. O'Riordan: **Catholicity And Progress In Ireland**, 1905, p324.

Because Ulster Custom was not based on a law, because the rights established for themselves by the Ulster tenants were not written down in a statute book, "any landlord who chose might disregard them". But any landlord who imagined that whatever was not an Act of Parliament did not exist was soon brought to his senses by the tenant farmers, who took the law into their own hands. A right is not an Act of Parliament but, as Marx put it, "an accomplished fact".

Nationalist historians represent this talking shop, Grattan's Parliament, as having achieved a profound and rapid transformation, not in the mere political structure of society, but in its *economy*. Now, it is obvious that it much more difficult to bring about economic development, than to bring about political reforms. And the very remarkable thing about Grattan's Parliament is that, while supposedly achieving extensive economic development, it failed to bring about democratic political changes for which there was a pressing demand.

Here is the Sinn Fein view of the matter:
"Grattan's Parliament was able to revive and stimulate Irish trade and commerce to a degree of prosperity which it had not enjoyed for centuries, because Grattan's Parliament was the sole fiscal authority in Ireland... Grattan's Parliament found Ireland a sheep-farm and a cattle-ranch, importing the bread it ate, and in a few years it transformed Ireland into a tillage country, feeding on its own corn and exporting the surplus. Fosters Corn Laws founded on the system of bounties worked the transformation... Grattan's Parliament in five years turned Ireland into a large exporter of manufactured goods and sent these goods under the Irish flag in a home-owned mercantile marine. This was possible because Grattan's Parliament controlled the Customs. In the less than 20 years existence Grattan's parliament converted Ireland from a pasturage to tillage, revived her greatness as a manufacturing nation, made her fisheries amongst the richest in the world, equipped herself with a mercantile marine and secured recognition in every part of Europe for the mercantile flag of Ireland" (**Sinn Fein**, 16.12.1911).

The economic development of Ulster, in particular, is attributed to the Irish Parliament (even before it became 'Grattan's Parliament' and acquired legislative independence). In 1919, when Sinn Fein should have been dealing rigorously with historical realities in an effort to establish common ground with Ulster Unionism, it retreated further into fantasy. It attempted to make Ulster feel obliged to the Irish Parliament for its industrial development:
"That [linen] manufacture in Ulster owes everything to the Irish Parliament. When the woollen manufacture was prohibited in the South by the jealousy of England, the linen manufacture was encouraged in Ulster by the Irish Parliament." (Nationality 17.2.1918.)

This attempt to convince Ulster that it owed its industrial development to the Irish Parliament cut very little ice in industrial Ulster, which knew perfectly well that it owed its industrial development mainly to itself.

It is true that there was a period of superficially impressive economic development, which partially coincided with the period of Grattan's Parliament. The two periods overlapped. The cycle of economic development began *before* Grattan's Parliament... and came to an end before the Union. By misrepresenting this overlap as a perfect coincidence of the two periods, and by assuming the coincidence to imply a cause and effect relationship (with the Parliament being the cause), Nationalist propaganda has been able to disseminate the notion that the Parliament brought about the economic development and that the Union destroyed it.

When the article, **Economics And Partition**, was published in 1967, this view of Grattan's Parliament was almost universally propagated by the Southern bourgeois intelligentsia. Though it was refuted in Gill's history of the linen industry, and in Connolly's Labour In Irish History, these refutations were without influence. Gill's book was not publicised, while Connolly's refutation was classified among his mistakes, even by 'Communists' who proclaimed themselves his followers. These 'Communists' took up the Nationalist myth of the far-reaching economic power of Grattan's Parliament, and a historically factual view of the matter was categorised as "ultra-leftist".

There have been significant changes since then. Having moved into the era of free trade, the Southern bourgeoisie needs to free itself from some of the old protectionist mythology. A new school of economic historians has emerged who deal in a more factual way with the economics of the Grattan's Parliament period, notably Raymond Crotty and L.M. Cullen.

In the legislative view of history, the growth of tillage in the second half of the 18th century was a miraculous effect of Foster's Corn Law (1784), giving bounties on corn exports. But Crotty (in **Irish Agricultural Production**) shows that the growth of tillage had economic causes:

"Between 1760... and 1815... changes of immense social significance took place in Irish agriculture. From the position of being a heavy corn importer during the middle of the 18th century, Ireland spectacularly increased her exports and reduced her imports till she became at the close of the period a substantial net exporter of corn" (p19).

"While increased agricultural output may have owed something to the legal reforms it is clear that overwhelmingly the increased output came in response to an increased demand which caused prices to rise after a prolonged period of stability or even falling prices, in the first half of the 18th century." (p21.)

"Foster's Corn Law of 1784... can hardly have failed to have had an impact and no doubt led to some quickening of production and exports. Against this, however, it is worth recalling that Irish corn production... had been recovering since 1758, when net imports reached their maximum, and that the country had become a net exporter of corn, flour and meal by 1783, before Foster's Corn Law... The significance of Foster's Corn Law has probably been greatly exaggerated. It was passed at a time when tillage was in any case recovering and corn exports expanding. It probably encouraged an increase in tillage and corn exports, which would almost certainly have occurred in any case...

"Foster's Corn Law has traditionally been regarded as one of, if not the, most important legislative measures taken by Grattan's Parliament to boost the Irish economy. No comparable measures were taken with regard to the dairy and pig industries, yet expansion in both of these industries appears to have been no less dramatic than in the case of corn production. Here there can be no question of expansion and prosperity being due to action by the Irish Parliament.

"Writing some forty years after the achievement of Irish independence and with the hindsight not afforded to O'Brien of the limitations on the capacity of Irish legislators to improve economic conditions, it is difficult not to agree with Connolly that at the period in question the decisive factor in stimulating the Irish economy was the application of new technology and the subsequent quickening of trade, particularly the growth of British demand. The influence of Grattan's Parliament was, if any, probably marginal." (p22-3.)

Grattan's Parliament not only lacked executive power, but it was not even a bourgeois Parliament in any effective sense. It was elected on a very narrow franchise. A majority of its members represented pocket boroughs, which were owned by Ascendancy aristocrats. It was a corrupt landlord Parliament. It refused to bring about democratic reforms in its own electoral base, not to mention bringing about democratic reforms in property relations. Far from causing a dramatic industrial development, which would have been beyond the power of a much more substantial political institution, it refused even to carry out reforms which were in its power, but were not in its interest. Land reform was the pressing economic need. But Grattan's Parliament was solidly against land reform.

George O'Brien, the main apologist for Grattan's Parliament, who maintains that it achieved miraculous results in the development of industry and agriculture, admits that it did not even attempt to carry out elementary land reform:

"The causes of Irish misery were very largely inherent in the land system and nothing less than a radical reform of that system could have succeeded in materially improving the condition of the smaller tenants and the agricultural labouring class. The reform of the Irish land system has been effected in recent years," [Mr. O'Brien does not add: 'by a Unionist government'], "and anybody conversant with the numerous difficulties, both economic and financial, which had to be overcome before that reform was carried through will readily admit that such a course of legislation would have been quite beyond the resources of Grattan's Parliament. The principles on which the new land system of Ireland was ultimately settled were totally alien to the 18th century conceptions—and the evils of the Irish land tenures were utterly beyond the power of the Irish Parliament to remedy" (Economic History Of 18th Century, p410-11).

In fact, the principles on which the land system was restructured within the Union were far from being "alien to 18th century conceptions". They existed not merely as conceptions, but as actual property relations, in Ulster. They were part of the programme of reforms of the United Irish bourgeoisie. And tenant right had long been established in England. It was not the novelty of the conception, or the difficulty in its implementation, that held Grattan's Parliament back from land reform on the basis of tenant-right: it was class interest. Grattan's Parliament represented the rack-renting landlord interest. The few democrats who penetrated it could only engage in impotent speechmaking. The bourgeois democracy of Ireland witnessed its passing with indifference. Some of the leading United Irish democrats, in prison for attempting to overthrow Grattan's Parliament, welcomed the Union as offering the only hope of democratic reform after the suppression of the United Irishmen. There is no reason to suppose that the extensive democratic reform carried out within the Union during the 19th century would have been carried out if Ireland had continued to be governed by the corrupt Ascendancy Parliament that was induced to liquidate itself in 1800.

O'Brien records that this Parliament was true to itself to the end:—
> "Possibly the greatest injustice which disgraced the (tithe) system in Ireland was the exemption of pasture land from tithes. The pasture land of the country was usually the property of rich land-owners or large graziers... There was no doubt that pastureland was legally liable to tithes."

But the gentry appealed to Parliament for an exemption and got it. But this exemption had been passed only by the House of Commons.
> "One of the last Acts of the Irish Parliament before its dissolution was to legalise the exemption of pasture land from tithes, as it was feared that the Executive of a United Kingdom might not be inclined to pay attention to the resolutions which had been passed by a single house of the Irish Parliament." (p146-7.)

Appendices

1. Greaves It is natural that Connolly's mistakes (particularly his Catholic Nationalist view of Ulster Unionism) should have been made into virtues by the Southern bourgeoisie, and that his scientific analyses (e.g., of Grattan's Parliament) should be represented as mistakes. And it is a sign of the success of the Southern bourgeoisie in influencing the working class movement that 'socialists' and 'Communists', with the exception of the B&ICO, should have mirrored this bourgeois approach to Connolly. When the B&ICO demonstrated, in the mid sixties, that Connolly's view of Grattan's Parliament was correct, the opportunists put it down as 'ultra-leftism'. The leading opportunist historian, C.D. Greaves, in his biography of Connolly, declared this to be "Connolly's weak point".

He provided no concrete historical analysis to support this view. When the B&ICO refuted it with concrete historical analysis, his only reply was that his view was identical with Marx's, while the view of Connolly and the B&ICO was at variance with Marx.

But the issue, of course, is not whose views agree with who's, but which view is historically accurate. There is no doubt that Marx's views, outlined in a few sketchy lecture notes, are incorrect. There is also no doubt that Marx never made any independent investigation of the matter. For the purpose of giving lectures in support of the Repeal of the Union in the 1860s, he took at their face value some O'Connellite statistics. The case for Repeal rested on contemporary issues and not on historical grounds. Marx's sketchy account of history is misleading, and he had nothing whatever to say about the different development of Ulster.

The opportunist view of Grattan's Parliament is changing as a consequence of the change on the part of bourgeois economic history. **The Formation Of The Irish Economy** (a collection edited by L.M. Cullen) was reviewed in the **Irish Democrat** (January 1971). The reviewer repeated (in a respectful tone of voice), that
> "the consensus... is that neither economic expansion in the 18th century nor contraction in the 19th can be understood wholly or even chiefly the result of political events. They are unanimously against the traditional view that Grattan's Parliament rescued the country from prolonged depression."

While opportunism is impervious to Marxist analysis, it is highly amenable to suggestion by the bourgeoisie.

2. Trotskyists Whatever agitational differences may exist between the Khruschevites and Trotskyists (or "revolutionary socialists") both agree in pushing the Catholic nationalist myths: "In the South the Union had the expected effects. The carefully fostered industries collapsed and the brief prosperity of the Grattan's Parliament era disappeared." (M. Farrell, People's Democracy leader, **Northern Star**, No. 5, p25). Of course, no evidence whatever is given about these "carefully fostered industries".

3. Gladstone And Unionists This was also the view of a British Prime Minister in the hey-day of the Empire. On March 28th, 1893 Gladstone lectured a delegation from the Belfast Chamber of Commerce on the "immense prosperity and advancement of Ireland during the period of an independent Parliament."

But the Chamber of Commerce delegation (which included descendants of the people who had attempted to overthrow Grattan's Parliament in the 1790s in the interests of political and economic progress) were unimpressed. They replied to Gladstone (April 11, 1893):

"We are the descendants of the Volunteers, and we inherit their traditions; we know what were their aims and aspirations... But we cannot accept the favourable view of the success of Grattan's Parliament... The undoubted advance in the material prosperity of Ireland during the earlier years of that Parliament's existence, was not attributable to its influence. It was due to causes in operation years before its independence... and altogether outside its sphere."

4. Walter MacDonald The Catholic Nationalist mythology relating to Grattan's Parliament and the Union was, during its heyday, challenged from within Catholic bourgeois nationalist politics by a solitary figure, Rev. Walter MacDonald, a Maynooth theologian, and a uniquely substantial intellectual in the history of the Southern bourgeois intelligentsia. MacDonald challenged the mythology in **Some Ethical Questions Of Peace And War**, published in 1919. In 1920, he published a "Postscript" to the above, in which he replied to a Sinn Fein criticism of it. The Sinn Fein criticism, published in the **Catholic Times** of November 22, 1919, set out to defend with historical argument the notion that the Union had caused the decay of Irish industry. MacDonald comments:

"...with the little knowledge that I had, I was puzzled, as I still am, by the historical statements which I had been hearing on all sides, from the propagandists of Sinn Fein; who, though assuming knowledge of the subject, and dogmatising vehemently, seemed to me to contradict my schoolbooks," [written presumably with a Unionist bias]. "And as they were written by men of some competence in the subject, I thought I should set expert against expert. Even schoolboys have a right, and should be encouraged, to do that."

The Sinn Fein method of criticism, says MacDonald, consists in finding some errors of detail and representing this as the main content of an argument. These errors,

"however trivial... will serve as specimens; the whole work you will say, is of a piece. Call the error puerile, or such as could disgrace a schoolboy; and await with confidence the applause of Sinn Fein gallery. The 'belittler of the motherland', professor though he is, is shown up for an ignoramus, and his book as worthless throughout. No bad method... of appeal to such a gallery.

But that a whole group of able men should have recourse to it, against a colleague, in what should be a quest for truth!"

"I thought that I could find other causes of the decay [of industry around the time of the Union]; I felt that... I should, in fairness, test those sweeping statements of fact in the light of what little knowledge I possessed. That, unfortunately, is my habit—I am built that way; unable to accept comfortably general statements of fact or theory, which seem to conflict with others to which I cannot shut my eyes. Were it otherwise, I might be recognised as a master, not a schoolboy." (p15.)

The Sinn Fein argument was that industry decayed and the population declined as a result of the Union and acts of oppression by the British government. The acts of economic oppression cited in the reply to MacDonald were: a) in 1820 trading between Cork and Jamaica was forbidden; b) in 1830 the export of Irish home-grown tobacco was forbidden; c) in 1832 a fine of £100 was imposed on anyone found in possession of home grown tobacco.

MacDonald pointed out that the population, in fact, *grew*, for more than forty years after the Union. "And all the while Belfast prospered, besides other towns in the North. They must have been allowed to trade with Jamaica: or perhaps they were privileged to grow and export tobacco" (p17).

"Is not the failure of Irish commerce too tragic to be ascribed in this way to the fact, if true, that Cork was not allowed to import rum from Jamaica, or the whole country to grow and export tobacco? Yet, it is these items which the syndicate [i.e., of Sinn Fein critics] have been able to add to the sum of our knowledge of British tyranny.

"I thought, at first, I might leave it at that... but distrust of these learned critics prevailed, and I did make some inquiries. With the result, which did not surprise me, that the tobacco grievance turns out to be a fine specimen of mare's nest. In the 12th and 15th years of the reign of Charles II (1672-1675), the growth of that plant was forbidden throughout the British Isles; but these laws were repealed, as regards Ireland, in the 20th year of the reign of George III (1780). Three or four years after this the prohibition was extended to Scotland with important modifications; so that from then till 1831, Scotland and Ireland were brought into uniformity with England...

"As regards the trade of Cork and Jamaica, I have not been able to ascertain particulars. The critics, of course, gave none; nor were they eager to supply them. When I asked a reference from one who threw this Jamaica outrage at me, he said he knew it only from the others; and though, when pressed, he promised to get a reference, it has not come so far. From which I suspect that it is another mare's nest." (p17.)

Among the observations made by MacDonald, the following is very much to the point: "After so many centuries of the clan system... it is no wonder that it should take some time to make us business men." (p24.)

Miscellany

Solow The importance of tenant-right as a cause of the greater economic development of Ulster is denied in a number of recent bourgeois economic histories. One of these is **The Land Question & The Irish Economy, 1870-1903**, by Barbara Lewis Solow (Harvard University Press, 1971). Regarding Ulster Custom, Mrs. Solow observes:

> "...it was never the case the Ulster landlords had no power to increase rent, and Ulster rents moved in some measure with the rise and fall of prices and land values. What was specified was that the rent was 'fair'".

Where a "fair" rent could not be agreed between landlord and tenant, firms who specialised in valuation were called in. And it was only while the tenant agreed to pay the "fair" rent that he was secure against eviction. Therefore:

> "It turns out that he has not got fixity of tenure at all... Fixity of tenure where rent is free to vary is fixity in a very restricted sense... There is nothing in the *institutional arrangement* called Ulster Custom that guarantees a fixity of tenure, and whether Ulster tenants (or Southern tenants) had fixity of tenure is an empirical question" (p24-5).

It isn't clear what Mrs. Solow means by "the *institutional arrangement* called Ulster Custom". The Custom evolved in a scandalously "empirical" way. As to "fixity of tenure": William Sharman Crawford, who campaigned for the legalisation of tenant right from the 1820s onwards, said in his evidence to the Devon Commission: "the term 'fixity of tenure' is one which conveys ideas so vague to my mind, that I hardly know what answer to give to it. It is not a term which I have ever used myself, with reference to my Bill."

It is obvious that fixity of tenure which is not conditional on paying rent is in fact ownership. It is an ambiguous term, and it appears to have been used in an ambiguous way by the Land League and the Nationalist Party in the South, when the tenants' movement was becoming a movement for absolute ownership, which served a nationalist purpose by being directed against the Ascendancy landlords.

Mrs. Solow observes that "rackrent" merely means "competitive rent", and that the landlords were inhibited from charging competitive rents by terrorism. She recognises two components in tenant-right: compensation for unexhausted improvements, and "pure tenant-right", or the right to occupy the land. When the outgoing tenant sells the right to occupy the land to the incoming tenant, he is charging for the difference between the competitive or rack rent and the "fair" rent.

> "...if the outgoing tenant sells his tenant right for what it will bring at auction, he is playing the rack-renting landlord to the incoming tenants. It is a wonder that such outgoing tenants were not denounced for avarice" (p28-9).

While this shows that Mrs. Solow's philanthropic bourgeois intellectual heart is in the right place, it doesn't say much for her grasp of political economy. It was entirely advantageous to economic development that the farmers should establish rights for themselves on the land, and eventually replace the landlords as the owners of the land. This was not because the farmers were kinder people than the landlords: if anything, the contrary was the case. There was a fair number of philanthropic landlords who sometimes let the kindness of their hearts (or the weakness of their economic power) moderate their demands. But the philanthropic farmer is a rare bird. He has not the large resources of the landlord. He acts more exclusively out of economic interest than the landlord. He is a harder employer of labour than the landlord. He is also more productive than the landlord, therefore the farmer class of the 20th century has greater economic power than the landlord class of the 19th.

When, as a tenant, he began to establish property rights for himself on the land, he made every effort to sell those rights for their value, and landlord interference was resented. The tenant-farmer class did not see the landlord who tried to put restrictions on the sale of tenant-right as their protector against rack-rent. The sale of tenant-right at its market price was *not* rack-rent; it was not rent at all. In the tenant-right market the farmers bought and sold the part in the ownership of the land that had been acquired by their class. Mrs. Solow's confusing of this with rent is mere moralising.

The following are her remarks about the connection between Ulster Custom and the general economic development of Ulster:

"The prosperity of Ulster as compared with the South has been frequently attributed to the existence of Ulster custom, but the explanatory value of the custom in this connection turns out to be a very slender reed indeed. In the first place there is no evidence of greater prosperity in Ulster until some two centuries after the custom was introduced." (p30.)

She quotes Arthur Young's remarks on the disgraceful condition of farming in Ulster, e.g., the farms were "nothing but patches for the convenience of weavers", and comments:

"The picture of a thriving Ulster agriculture, accumulating capital under the beneficent Ulster custom and investing it in improved techniques, does not belong to the 18th century when Ulster was covered with tiny holdings of weavers so impoverished that they needed the yields of primitive agriculture to bring their pitifully small earnings from weaving up to subsistence level. That these weavers accumulated enough capital in their condition to finance the growth of the linen industry and eventually the Industrial Revolution in Ulster is not credible. For the rise of the linen industry we shall probably do better to look to the Huguenots who came to the North in the early decades of the 18th century... It is true that the linen industry was *based* upon the weaver-farmer, without whose willingness to provide woven cloth at a less-than-living wage the industry could not be developed. My feeling is that in the South, in the plains of the Midlands, the dairylands of Limerick, and the corn counties of the Southeast, the tenant would have been ill-advised to turn to weaving: it promised him no riches. In one sense it can be viewed almost as an accident that the Industrial Revolution eventually flourished among the descendants of the Ulster weavers and providential that most of Ulster's soil was too poor to support permanent grassland without careful management by methods unknown in the 18th century. The prosperity of Ulster agriculture rose with the departure of the weaver from the countryside" (p30-2).

It seems that Mrs. Solow's book is considered as offering some comfort to the Catholic nationalist view of history, but we have not yet been able to grasp why this is so. What is obvious is that she does not deal at all in political economy— in the evolution of property relations. "Poverty", for example, is not a category of political economy. Two people may be equally poor, but yet be involved in entirely different production relations.

She says that it "is not credible" that the weavers should have accumulated the capital to launch the industrial revolution. She doesn't show where the capital came from, but says it was "probably" the Huguenots. But it is notorious that there was no shortage of money capital in Southern Ireland at the time of the industrial revolution. Southern money was being invested abroad while the home economy stagnated. The problem was not a shortage of free money, but a lack of reasonably safe investment opportunities. Capital is not merely money, but a social relationship, as Marx never tired of emphasising. In the South of Ireland, there was plenty of free money, but an absence of the necessary social and technical conditions for capitalist development. But the broadly based market development in the North in the 18th century had created the social conditions required for industrial capitalism. The mere money element came, no doubt, from many different sources.

Mrs. Solow explains nothing about social development. It is appropriate that she should invoke 'accident' and 'providence'. The notion that the industrial development of the North was an accidental consequence of the fact that the land wasn't good enough for farming fits well into the Catholic Nationalist mythology. With this approach, the development of capitalism, economically and politically, in England would be represented as the most fantastic chapter of accidents that the world has ever seen.

[This section exists because of Paul Bew (now Professor Bew), with whom I used to discuss these matters extensively between 1970 and 1972. I doubt that I would ever have read Solow's book if he had not insisted that it was enormously important. I read it and found it trivial, and Bew could not explain to me how it struck at the foundations of the Ulster Custom argument. I later realised that, because I have no connection with the academic world, or the world of commercial publishing, and am not wealthy, it is not advantageous to anybody hoping to make an academic career to be associated with me. Academia has become a trade organised as a closed shop and I am a maverick producer on the outside spoiling things for it. I imagine that the importance of Solow arose in that context as a kind of diplomatic toothache. Anyhow, Bew ceased to have anything to do with me very soon after getting me to read Solow, though I cannot recall that we ever came to any definite disagreement. BC, Note to 1992 edition.]

Cullen Another economist, who is being increasingly referred to by those who are attempting to salvage the Sinn Fein view of history is L.M. Cullen. Cullen's most comprehensive book so far is **An Economic History Of Ireland Since 1660** (1972). Cullen pioneered the new school of free trade economists in the South. The job of these economists is to refute the economic ideology of the protectionist era and to develop an economic ideology for the free trade era. Cullen, therefore, is self-consciously iconoclastic in respect of the George O'Brien/Sinn Fein ideology concerning the effects of legislation on trade and economic development. In this book he writes, for example, that "it is hard to see how the Irish woollen industry could have increased its exports significantly in the 18th century, or how the industry could have acquired a potential for transforming the Irish economy. The act of 1699 emerges as irrelevant in the main to the central problems of the first decade of the 18th century" (p42). He also refutes the idea that Grattan's Parliament built up Irish industry and that the Union destroyed it.

But his scientific approach goes no further than that. The Southern ruling class has abandoned protectionism, but not its claim on the North. And Cullen writes nothing in his Economic History to upset the one-nation ideology. He does not deal at all with the economic basis of the Partition conflict.

He asserts that the linen industry revived in the South in the 1780s, after the economic crisis which wiped out the centralised linen production of the South in the 1770s. But it revived in a different form. It

"was no longer centralised. The initiative for expansion came largely from the people themselves. Not only is this a feature throwing doubt on the proposition that religious factors may have influenced the evolution of the linen industry, but it also casts doubt on an associated factor, the widely held assumption that the land system had encouraged the industry in the north through greater security of tenure and discouraged it in the rest of the island. The growth of the industry in the 1780s was especially pronounced in the poorer regions. In Co. Kerry for instance, the value of linen sales had been only £400 in 1770; in 1800 output was valued at £56,000. More remarkable still was Co. Mayo... The significance of the linen industry lies in the fact that it was not confined to Ulster but was far flung in the island, increasingly so as the century went by" (p62-3).

He gives no explanation of how the industry was organised in Kerry and Mayo, what long term social effects it had, or what happened to it. He just gives a couple of trade statistics (and those who are influenced by him imagine that economic history is tables of trade statistics). Later, he says: "The linen industry was now beginning to concentrate in the north-east, its growth after 1825 reflecting a very buoyant level of economic activity around Belfast" (p108). The flourishing peasant industry of Kerry and Mayo is mentioned no more.

The Southern economy in this period (like Cullen's history) was something of a patchwork. In very favourable market conditions, spurts of economic development of various kinds were achieved in various localities, usually being stimulated by public spirited landlords. A number of Nationalist economists make reference to these to demonstrate that there was a unified national economy in Ireland, and no significant economic difference between North and South, and that is all that Cullen does. But fragmentary spurts of development, which usually petered out in a short while, do not bear comparison with the comprehensive and sustained economic development of the North. (In the South, it was only the Quakers, those pure personifiers of the capitalist world outlook, those "meek and money making followers of George Fox", to use William Cobbett's words, who sustained a continuous economic development throughout the 18th and 19th centuries: and the Quakers were not a nucleus, but a marginal element, in Southern society.)

Lenin On Land Tenure The following passage from Lenin's **Development Of Capitalism In Russia** has been cited in support of the view that the land system was not particularly significant in the development of capitalism:

"It is a great mistake to think that the inception of agricultural capitalism itself requires some special form of land tenure. 'But the form of landed property with which the incipient capitalist mode of production is confronted does not suit it. It first creates for itself the form required by subordinating agriculture to capital. It thus transforms feudal landed property, clan property, small-peasant property in work communes—no matter how divergent their juristic forms may be—into the economic form corresponding to the requirement of this mode of production' (Capital. Vol 3, p2). Thus, by the very nature of the case, no peculiarities in the system of land tenure can serve as an insurmountable obstacle to capitalism, which assumes different forms in accordance with the different conditions in agriculture, legal relationships and manner of life...

"That is why we are very indifferent to the question of the form of peasant land tenure... The really important question concerns not the form of land tenure at all, but the remnants of the purely mediaeval past, which continue to weigh down upon the peasantry." (Ch. 4, Section XI.)

If it was being argued that there was a homogeneous society in Ireland in the early 17th century, and that this unified society was subsequently divided by the passing of different land laws for the North and the South—that capitalism developed in the North due to favourable land laws, and that it was prevented from developing in the South because of unfavourable laws—it would be very much to the point to cite this statement of Lenin's in criticism of that view. But that is not how the B&ICO have treated the matter. (George O'Brien and his trotskyist and modern revisionist followers, however, do frequently treat it like that.)

The B&ICO has emphasised that it was social, not legal, differences that caused the uneven development of capitalism. Ulster Custom is not a product of legislation, but a product of class struggle which was outside the law until 1870. Our historical starting point is not some abstract legality, but the actual fact of two separate and qualitatively different communities which existed in Ireland in the 17th century, and we have attributed their maintenance as separate communities mainly to the differences in the economic development of each of them. And we have attributed this difference in economic development chiefly to their internal social structures.

Land tenure turns out to be an ambiguous term, by which can be meant either a piece of legislation, or a production relationship, or both. But Ulster Custom can only be a production relationship. It had no legal existence. Where capitalist production relationships are developing in the economy, they can modify pre-capitalist legal forms to suit their needs. Ulster Custom is, in fact, a case in point where a production relationship developed against the law, and forced the law to bend.

Feudalism? Following the military defeat of the Gaelic clan aristocracy in 1603, Chichester decreed the abolition of feudalism in Ireland in 1605. The social order of the clans was described as feudal. With the abolition of feudal ties, the clan peasantry were to be freed from personal bondage to the chiefs, and were to become a free peasantry bound only by contractual relations to their landlords.

Almost three hundred years later, Michael Davitt wrote a history of the Land League, which he entitled **The Fall Of Feudalism In Ireland**. In this period, the development of peasant proprietors certainly established bourgeois society firmly in the Southern countryside. But how is the rural economy of the South to be characterised from 1605 to the 1880s? Lenin wrote as follows about the rural economy of Russia after the abolition of serfdom in the 1860s:

"...the attempts of some landlords, immediately after the Reform, to import machinery and even workers from abroad could not but end in a fiasco... Capitalist economy could not emerge at once, and corvee economy could not disappear at once. The only possible system of economy was, accordingly, a transitional one, a system combining the features of both the corvee and the capitalist systems... With all the endless variety of forms characteristic of a transitional epoch, the economic organisation of contemporary landlord farming amounts to two main systems, in the most varied combinations—the labour-service system and the *capitalist* system. The first consists in the landlord's land being cultivated with the implements of the neighbouring peasants... The capitalist farming system consists of the hire of workers who till the land with the owner's implements. The systems mentioned are actually interwoven in the most varied and fantastic fashion; on a mass of landlord estates there is a combination of the two systems..."

"Life creates forms that unite in themselves with remarkable gradualness systems of economy whose basic features constitute opposites" (Development Of Capitalism In Russia, Chapter 3, Section 2).

In Ireland, likewise, transitional forms, combining features of different modes of production, came into being in the 17th (or even 16th) century. In the South, these transitional forms continued for more than two centuries, and were subject to great local variation. Features of clan, feudal, and capitalist economy were mixed together in it. In Ulster, the existence of a strong tenant-farmer class, actively engaged in simple commodity production, ensured the bourgeoisification of the landlords, and caused a strong capitalist economic, social and political development. Elsewhere, the absence of a vigorous tenant-farmer class involved in market relations led to the rack-rent landlord system, which was organised in a variety of ways. The landlords, who might incline towards the bourgeois world under British influence, or towards the feudal world under the influence of the opportunity to do so which was open to them, were described by Engels as a "lumpen" gentry.

Two Kinds Of Capitalist Development Marx describes two different ways in which capital enters the life of a society:

"The transition from the feudal mode of production is two-fold. The producer becomes merchant and capitalist, in contrast to the natural agricultural economy and guild-bound handicrafts of the mediaeval urban industries. This is the really revolutionising path. Or else, the merchant establishes direct sway over production. However much this serves historically as a stepping-stone... it cannot by itself contribute to the overthrow of the old mode of production... Without revolutionising the mode of production, it only worsens the condition of the direct producers, turns them into mere wage workers and proletarians under conditions worse than those under the immediate control of capital, and appropriates their surplus value on the basis of the old mode of production." (**Capital**, Volume 3, p329.)

In Capital, Volume 1, Marx showed that the development of a fully fledged capitalist mode of production was not immediately preceded by a fully fledged feudal mode of production. The feudal system of production had disintegrated many centuries before capitalist production began. The mass of the people on the land had long ceased to be serfs.

"In England, serfdom had practically disappeared in the last part of the 14th century. The immense majority of the population consisted then, and to a still larger extent in the 15th century, of free peasant proprietors, whatever was the feudal title under which their right of property was hidden." (p717.)

In Ireland in the 18th and much of the 19th century, the two different ways in which capitalist production develops can be observed in action: in Ulster from the small producers; in the South from the intervention of merchants' capital: in Ulster with a revolutionising effect on society; in the South with a very different effect.

In Ulster in the 17th and 18th centuries, a market economy, soundly based on extensive small-commodity production in the countryside, developed. While the Ulster tenant farmers were not as free economically as the 15th century English peasantry, they were beyond all comparison more developed as a small commodity producing class than the peasantry of the South. In Ulster in the 18th century, capitalism was being developed from the small commodity base of society. But in the South, capitalist development was taking place from the top downwards. Investment from Britain went mostly to the South in the 18th century. In the 19th century, the vigorous capitalist economy of the North began to attract investment from outside. Outside investment had vastly different effects in the North and the South, due to the differences in the nature of the economy in which it was being invested. It was not until the latter half of the 19th century that the peasantry in the South became a force of small commodity producers generating capitalism.

But, in Ulster the development was not only earlier, but was much more thorough and freer from distorting influences, than in the South.

Ireland was first unified under the British administration. (The present unity of many previously heterogeneous areas derives from their position as British administrative units, e.g., many African countries.) All-Ireland national unity was later asserted by the Southern bourgeoisie. But the more the actual history of Ireland is investigated, the less tenable becomes the idea of a unity which was disrupted. This is particularly the case when popular forces are coming to the fore.

Ireland may have been a practical unit for the British administration, or for British merchants' capital, and there may have been a certain unity in the landlord class, but in the long run these proved to be overlays on the society. Beneath this overlay there were two quite different societies. And capitalism developed quite separately in each of these societies. The development of capitalism (a popular force relative to preceding modes of production), while disrupting the unity of the old colonial superstructure, merely asserted the division which had existed throughout at the popular level.

Theories Of Capitalist Development

The fact that in the 19th century Irish society had not yet evolved into a single national society expresses itself in the non-existence of anything resembling an economic or political history of Ireland as a whole in the 19th century. Catholic nationalist historians took the Catholic South to be the true Ireland, felt ideologically obliged to treat Irish society as being essentially of a kind throughout, and were therefore incapable of writing the history of Ulster. The industrial development of Ulster appears in their writings as an accidental and superficial phenomenon. Ulster Unionist historians, on the other hand, took the industrial development of Ulster to be the substantial reality of Irish society, and they tended to regard the South as a backward hinterland of Ulster which would eventually be drawn into the development pioneered by Ulster.

When the South, instead of behaving as the hinterland of industrial Ulster, developed a distinct national movement of its own, which threatened to swamp Ulster, Ulster Unionists were forced to take account of this development. For that reason, the Ulster Unionist movement came nearer to comprehending the reality of Ireland as a whole than did the Nationalist movement, which aspired to end the Unionist development of Ulster. It is still the case that Unionist Ireland is virtually incomprehensible to Nationalist Ireland, and this absence of comprehension often develops into the conviction that Unionist Ulster is insubstantial.

Historians of both camps assume that the Union had a uniform effect throughout Ireland. The Unionist view, therefore, is that it was generally beneficial, and the Nationalist view that it was generally harmful. For example: "The industrial history of Ireland during the 19th century shows how impossible it was for Irish manufactures to compete with British, once the two countries were commercially united" (Alice Murray: **Commercial Relations Between England And Ireland**). On the other hand, there is Henry Cooke's reply to O'Connell in the 1840s: "Look at Belfast, and be a Repealer if you can."

Thievery And Progress George O'Brien, having freely generalised to the effect that the Union was economically catastrophic for Ireland, felt obliged to glance at Belfast. And here is what he thought he saw (in his

Historical Introduction to **Modern Irish Trade And Industry**, by E.J. O'Riordan, 1920):

"To the general spectacle of industrial decay which Ireland presented in 1850 there was one fortunate exception, namely the northeast corner of Ulster. The progress of this one locality at a time when every other part of the country was declining is a remarkable phenomenon which calls for some explanation. In the 18th century Ulster stood in by no means the same position of industrial pre-eminence compared with the rest of Ireland which it occupies today. The linen industry, it is true, was more in evidence in the northern province than elsewhere, but it was no no means non-existent in the south and west; and with the exception of the newly established cotton industry, Ulster did not possess under Grattan's Parliament any undue share of the manufacturing wealth of the country. But in 1850 a great change had taken place; the linen industry was practically extinct in the three southern provinces, while it continued to flourish in Ulster; and by far the largest part of the cotton manufacture was carried on in the same district.

"Ulster, indeed, owes a far larger share of her industrial development to cotton than to linen manufacture. The cotton industry was the one industry that made substantial advances during the years following the Union, principally because it alone continued to be encouraged by protective duties. It was the localisation of this industry in Belfast... that conferred on Ulster the position of industrial importance which that province was destined to maintain for the remainder of the 19th century." (p42.)

And *why* did not the retention of cotton tariffs after the Union preserve the industry in the South? Why did the cotton industry develop in Ulster at the same time that it was declining in the South? O'Brien says "The reason that Ulster was enabled to progress during the period in which the remainder of Ireland declined was that the improved process of manufacture was adopted in the northern province." And *why* did technological development occur in Ulster, but not elsewhere? "Was this in any way due to the superior industrial character in Ulster," O'Brien asks. And, of course, he concludes that it was not:

"...the failure of the southern manufacturers to introduce improvements was due to their inability to amass capital owing to the land system; and it is equally the fact that the reason Ulster was enabled to progress was because capital could be accumulated owing to the essential difference in the land system in the north... Ulster Custom was undoubtedly the reason why the industries of Ulster weathered the storm which swept away those of the south and west." (p44.)

Assuming that North and South were industrially equal, how exactly did the land tenure prevent technological development in an already existing industry in the South, or bring it about in the North? And how could land tenure prevent capital accumulation in industry? Did the Northern cotton manufacturers accumulate out of profits made by tenant farmers (who were not involved in the cotton trade), rather than out of the surplus value created by the workers in industry? O'Brien gives no clue as to how he imagines it happened. Land tenure is introduced as the magical answer to everything.

Furthermore, he appears to conceive of land tenure in its legal aspect, rather than as a class relationship. Land law, however, was of a kind throughout Ireland. The only difference between north and south in this respect, lay in the ability of the tenant-farmers to force the landlords by class struggle to recognise certain rights for them on the land. So that "land tenure", in the sense of a production relationship, far from being a different thing to "industrial character", was very much an expression of "industrial character".

O'Brien does not mention at all, in this connection, that a vigorous, enterprising, industrial capitalist class had developed in Ulster, but had not developed in the South.

He mentions the frequency of strikes as another factor contributing to the decline of industry in the South. But he conceded that

"the strikes were... less often actuated by the desire to better the workers' conditions than by the fear of their position being lowered by reason of the decay of the industry which was taking place. The decline of an industry caused combination and strikes, which themselves operated only to hasten the decline... a vicious circle." (p46.)

However, he also comments:

"The most unpleasant feature of the strikes was that they were frequently directed from England, and it is impossible to resist the conclusion that an Irish worker was on some occasions used as a tool by English interests to injure Irish industry." (48.)

Tempting though this latter argument might be, it is obvious that Ulster industry was a much more serious competitor with British industry than Southern industry was, but the British capitalists weren't able to use the Ulster workers to decrease the efficiency of industry there. To pursue that approach, therefore, might lead back to a difference in "industrial character", and once that was admitted, the idea of the essential unity of Irish society would not long survive. So O'Brien concludes:

"The industrial decay of Ireland was caused... by no failing of character either on the part of the employer or of the workman, but was the result of the fiscal changes which were introduced at the Union, and completed twenty years later. The abolition of duties was vital, owing to the inability of Irish manufacturers to compete with their English rivals; and this inability was itself the result of the impossibility of capital being accumulated in Ireland under the land system as it then was. Ultimately, of course, the cause of the decay was political... the progress of Ulster, on the other hand, was the result of differences in the land system which prevailed in that province, and was in no way due to the Act of Union. In other words, the Union was responsible for the industrial decline of the south, but was in no way responsible for the industrial advance of the north. Indeed, it is very probable that north-east Ulster would have been even more prosperous today had the Union never been passed." (p50.)

Believe that, whoever can.

On the question of industrial character, O'Brien further argued that, far from being superior to the South in this respect, the North was inferior. But the very inferiority, with respect to industrial character, of people of the North worked to the industrial advantage of the North. And this is how it happened.

When the linen industry revived in Ulster, co-incident with the decline of the cotton industry, in the 1820s, it did not revive on its old basis of small commodity production, but as capitalist manufacturing industry.

"The principal improvements that were introduced into this branch of the industry were the cessation of the custom by which weavers supplemented their earnings by farming small portions of land, and the congregation of weavers into factories." This development "converted the former man of all trades into a skilled full time workman; and the institution of the factory

system also made for increased output and greater efficiency... It was said that the introduction of the improvement was encouraged by the widespread embezzlement of yarn which took place when the work was performed in the weavers' own homes" (p43-4).
Therefore:
"...the only way in which the special character of the Ulster people influenced the industrial development of the province was by hastening on the introduction of the factory system on account of their dishonesty in dealing with the yarn in their own home" (p45).

The only notice O'Brien takes of the Northern industrial capitalist class is in the following passage (on which it might be commented that Catholic nationalist economic 'history' leads to the conclusion that if the mountain of labour repeatedly brings forth a mouse in the South of Ireland, the tendency in the North is for the mouse to give birth to whole ranges of mountains):
"The remarkable growth of Belfast... is generally attributed to the financial difficulties of the Chichester family at the end of the 18th century. So great was their need of money that they granted away their Belfast estates in perpetuity in consideration of heavy fines, and thus the lands got into the hands of the commercial class, and away from the baneful influence of landlordism. 'To these perpetuity leases', says Mr. Godkin in "The Land War in Ireland", 'we must undoubtedly ascribe the existence of a middle class, and the accumulation of capital for manufacture and commerce.'" (p45-6.)
And *that* is one of the best efforts of Nationalist Ireland to understand Unionist Ireland.

R.R. Kane R.R. Kane's **The Industrial Resources Of Ireland** (1844) is often referred to by Nationalist writers as one of the first major documents of the industrial movement in the South of Ireland. The book is mainly a technical treatment of physical resources, but its last chapter deals with social matters. Kane's observations on these matters are very objective, and free of apologetics. On the matter of labour costs, for example, he remarked that, while wages were lower in Ireland than in England, so was productivity, and that "cheapness of labour is thus shewn to be quite different from the nominal rate of wages". There was also a great shortage of skilled labour in Ireland. The introduction of British workers, paid at a higher rate, proportionate to the greater intensity of their labour, was one source of the labour problems besetting industry in the South. The native workers tended to demand the same rate of pay as the British workers.
"Employers are in Ireland much less able to stand out against strikes than in the sister kingdom. They possess less capital; its rapid circulation is a matter of more pressing necessity, and hence any temporary interruption is more felt. But still more important is the circumstance, that in Ireland employers are more dependent on their men, than those of the same class in England. They do not in general know their own trade as well. If an English workman refuses to do a piece of work, the master can, if he chooses, do it himself, and this gives the employer a moral superiority and power, which the Irish manufacturer in too many cases, does not possess." (p405.)
Dealing with the argument that lack of capital led to lack of industry, R.R. Kane wrote:
"This has been the bugbear of Irish enterprise for many years. England has capital, Ireland has not; therefore, England is rich and industrious, and Ireland is poor and idle. But where was the capital when England began to

grow rich? It was the industry that made the capital, not the capital the industry." (p408.)

"When money is made in England, it is re-invested in the same or in a similar branch, concerns are increased, and transactions multiplied, until the amount of capital attains the vast dimension which we now see. If some money be made in trade in Ireland, it is not so treated, it is withdrawn from trade, and stock is bought, or land is bought, yielding only a small return, but one with the advantage of not requiring intense exertion or intelligence, and free from serious risk...; that capital of great amount does truly exist in Ireland available for industrial uses, if the owners had a taste therefor, is certain. More than two millions of Irish capital is transferred every year to England in purchase of English government stock" (p408-9).

"The fault is not in the country, but in ourselves; the absence of successful enterprise is owing to the fact, that we do not know how to succeed; we do not want activity, we are not deficient in mental power, but we want special industrial knowledge. England, which in absolute education and general morality is below us... is far above us in industrial knowledge. The man who knows not how to read or write, who has never been at church, who never taught his child to reverence the name of his creator, will be a perfect master of his trade...; from the task which he undertakes nothing will turn him aside; he knows that time as well as labour is required for an industrial result; his acquaintance with the probabilities of his trade prepares him for difficulties, and hence enables him to surmount them...

"An Irishman takes up a branch of trade; after a time he finds it requires more capital than he expected... He finds that the profits are less than he had hoped, or he discovers that for a long time he can make no profit, and he is discouraged. Circumstances arise which he is not prepared to meet; the conditions of the branch of industry may have changed since he first entered into it, and finally he loses, perhaps, all that he had embarked in trade, simply because he did not know his trade well enough." (p412-3.)

"If a man knows Greek or Latin... what does it avail him when he proceeds to spinning cotton, or smelting iron... His habits and modes of thought are at every moment shocked by the rough clashing of the realities on which his fate depends. His mind, accustomed to discussions, which, whether right or wrong, leave life as it has been before, becomes appalled at the stern calculations of a problem, in which his liberty, his home, his fortune is involved. The man is not able for his position, and he fails." (p415.)

Kane, by contrast with O'Brien, attributed the development of Ulster society to the "industrial character of the people":

"The linen manufacture has been, hitherto, almost exclusively confined to the north of Ireland. This does not arise from any physical circumstances of soil or climate, or from the greater facilities of access to mechanical power; on the contrary, the soil of Ulster, if we except the valley of the Lagan and some scattered districts, is not, by any means, equal to the soils of the south and centre. The growth of this department of industry in Ulster, is owing rather to moral causes. Its population was, essentially, of a class devoted to industrial pursuits, and eager after independence and power which pecuniary success confers, and which was within their reach; whilst in the south, the wretched remnants of feudal barbarism paralysed all tendency to improve. The lord was above industry; the slave below it; and hence, although the circumstances of a fertile soil, easy access to markets, and abundance of motive power, were, in themselves, favourable, the blessings which nature presented were left unutilized, by the ignorance and inertness of the people" (p338).

It is certain that no industrial development takes place in any other way than through the industrious activity of people, and that the Catholic nationalist attempt to devise an explanation of the industrial development of Ulster, which owes nothing to the industrial character of the people, is absurd.

Plunkett And The Catholic Church A controversy about this matter occurred at the beginning of the 20th century. Horace Plunkett, the originator of the agricultural co-operative movement, made the following observations in his book, **Ireland In The New Century** (1905):

"Unhappily it has been borne in upon me, in the course of a long study of Irish life, that our failure to rise to our opportunities and to give practical evidence of the intellectual qualities with which the race is admittedly gifted, was due to certain defects of character, not ethically grave, but economically paralysing. I need hardly say I refer to lack of moral courage, initiative, independence and self-reliance... defects which, however they may be accounted for, it is the first duty of modern Ireland to recognise and overcome." (pix.)

Plunkett attributed these defects to the action of the Penal Laws and the commercial restraints, which made industriousness a pointless exercise. Along with the decline of industriousness, there grew up a belief in the omnipotence of legislation; a belief which was prolonged by Nationalist politicians (who included a high percentage of lawyers):

"The people have an extraordinary belief in political remedies for economic ills, and their political leaders, who are not as a rule themselves actively engaged in business life, tell the people... that if they were allowed to apply their panacea, Ireland would quickly rebuild her industrial life." (p36.)

"The cause or cure of Irish ills", said Plunkett, were neither chiefly political nor religious, "whatever be the effect of Roman Catholic influence upon the practical side of the people's life" (p29). But he went on to remark that "Roman Catholicism strikes an outsider as being in some of its tendencies non-economic, if not actually anti-economic"; and that the "defect in the industrial character of Roman Catholics... however caused, seems to me to have been intensified by their religion." (p101-2.)

Though Plunkett's agricultural movement of the late 19th, and early 20th century, was the most substantial thing of its kind which had ever developed in Southern Ireland, and it gained widespread support from the farming class which was developing rapidly on the basis of land reform, it was strongly opposed by Home Rule politicians, because it did not base itself on nationalist politics, and limited itself strictly to economic policy. Plunkett quoted the following statement as exemplifying his remarks quoted above:

"Rathkeale is a Nationalist town... and every pound of butter made in its Creamery must be made on Nationalist principles..."

Plunkett did not regard the economic influence of Catholicism as being entirely negative in Ireland:

"Knowing as I do the part which religion plays in the life of Irish Roman Catholics, I rely upon their church to foster contentment under the comparatively low standard of physical comfort, and the limited range of industrial opportunity, which must prevail in Ireland while the new peasant proprietory is being constituted and organised." (p322.)

But, apart from this passive virtue, and while acknowledging the economic virtues of Catholicism in mediaeval times, he held the economic influence of Catholicism in modern Ireland to be a hindrance to the development of a vigorous capitalist economic outlook:

"The reliance of that religion on authority, its repression of individuality, and its complete shifting of what I may call the moral centre of gravity to a future existence... to mention no other characteristics... appear to me to be calculated, unless supplemented by other influences, to check the growth of the qualities of initiative and self-reliance..." (p102).

These remarks provoked a response in the form of a large volume, entitled **Catholicity and Progress In Ireland**, by the Rev. M. O'Riordan, which went through four editions in its first year of publication. But this refutation was in fact more in the nature of a justification. O'Riordan declared that: "Human progress and civilisation must not be identified with material progress; with gas, electricity, railroads and factories.: (4th ed. p60); and that "Even though I granted that Catholicism is an obstacle to industrial progress, there would be no ground for complaint unless it professed, or ought to have professed, to promote the temporal interests of man" (p46).

With regard to Catholic authoritarianism, O'Riordan declared that "Authority... is the safeguard of liberty of the subject." Any authority which is to inspire a sense of duty must be based on

"a religion which does not owe its power to the individuals whom it is supposed to guide. If it depends on the people to determine what doctrines it shall teach, it is only a religion of their own making which they may shape or discard at their will. Made by the people they can unmake it with equal right... To subject oneself to a religion of human manufacture like that is to bear the yoke of a religious despotism which a people can never venerate, and which they will not long endure at an inconvenience. Well, that is Protestantism precisely; for it assumes that God has ordered a religion; but instead of having to take charge of anybody, everybody has to take charge of it. Protestantism is essentially of home manufacture; each person makes his own according to his conviction or fancy." (p65.)

O'Riordan imagined that this refuted Plunkett: in fact, it merely contributed to Plunkett's argument.

It so happens that the nations which made capitalism dominant as a world system, and which made the bourgeois conception of freedom dominant in the world—Holland, England, Scotland, Switzerland, America, North Germany—were Protestant nations. Along with developing a new mode of production and a new conception of liberty, these nations also made their own religions. The Roman monopoly was replaced by a vigorous home manufacture. And having made their own religions, these nations went on to develop a non-religious conception of the world. What began with Luther, Calvin, Knox and the House of Commons making up their own religions, led to Professor Huxley who, says Rev. O'Riordan, "held that his ideas budded from his brain by the same law under which flowers blossom on the rose-bush, or heads of cabbage grow in a garden" (p99).

(Or, as Dr. Kane put it, Watt, who invented the steam engine, never troubled his brain with Latin, until he felt the need of it for business purposes.)

Rev. O'Riordan, taking a high moral tone, said that he was not

"as a Catholic, at all concerned to prove that Catholicism is better or even equal to non-Catholicism of any kind in the matter of trade, commerce, manufactures, or making money" (p169).

Affecting a lofty contempt of Belfast, he observed:

"Of literary life, there is a painful absence... It has not produced even a respectable newspaper or magazine. Of art, they seem to have little conception. The practical life they live unfits them for the ideal. I suppose it is a sign of the 'economic sense'." (p245.)

Rev. O'Riordan delicately hints at how the people of industrial Ulster, who are immune to the fine things of life, occupy themselves culturally:

"It seems that Orangeism and illegitimacy go together, and that bastards in Ireland are in proportion to the Orange Lodges" ... "The highest in their order of unchastity [that is, as manifested in illegitimate births] are:- Antrim 5.8%; Armagh 5.0%; Londonderry 4.8%; Down 4.5%; Tyrone 4.0%; Fermanagh 3.5%; Monaghan 2.8%; Donegal 2.0%; Cavan 1.6%. In Connaught... the average of illegitimate births is 0.9. Let us consider the meaning of these figures. In 1,000 persons in Banff, Scotland, there are 171 bastards... —in Antrim 58 bastards—in Leitrim 6 bastards" (p272.)

These facts, of course, would mean different things in different circumstances. But in the 20th century, if it could be demonstrated that there was a necessary connection between the fact that Protestant Antrim was the stronghold of heavy industry in Ireland and the fact that it was also the stronghold of 'bastardom', the effect would not be to make heavy industry a vice, but to make bastardom a virtue. And for all Rev. O'Riordan's affectation of confidence in mediaeval virtue, it can be distinctly sensed that he feels the tide is running against him, and that the future lies with Antrim's virtue rather than with Leitrim's.

Medaevalism Even George O'Brien, the flower of Nationalist political economy, had grafted modern bourgeois economic theory onto a mediaeval conception of the world. He expressed his general world outlook in **The Economic Effects Of The Reformation** (1923). In his view, the great catastrophe in history was the Reformation. But for the Reformation, the Catholic Church would have achieved the general industrial development of society, while keeping society (or at least European society) together as a great, harmonious, whole. It would have achieved all that was good in the achievements of capitalism, while avoiding all that was evil, and would have thereby prevented the development of socialism.

The source of all economic evil was the Protestant heresy. The characteristics of the earlier heretical sects "had been world-renunciation and asceticism, while those of the new sects in Protestant countries were extreme individualism." (p27.)

The Catholic Church was making provision for the freeing of individual initiative, within certain limits, under the guidance and control of the Church. But the Reformation broke the power of the Church at the critical moment, and opened the way for the development of unrestrained individualism, which led in turn to the development of a socialist movement. Therefore, "both capitalism and socialism alike can be shown to have their common origin in the Protestant Reformation." (p67.)

(Or, as he expressed it in another work, Ricardo and Marx were "two Jews tugging at the same rotten rope", **The Phantom Of Plenty**, p50.)

"Capitalism found its roots in the intensely individualistic spirit of Protestantism, in the spread of anti-authoritative ideas from the realm of religion into the realm of political and social thought, and above all, in the distinctive Calvinist doctrine of a successful and prosperous career being the outward and visible sign by which the regenerated might be known. Socialism, on the other hand, derived encouragement from the violations of established and prescriptive rights of which the Reformation afforded so many examples, from the growth of heretical sects tainted with Communism, and from the overthrow of the orthodox doctrine of original sin, which opened the way to the idea of the perfectibility of men through institutions." (p171.)

He laments the disruption of Catholic mediaevalism, and looks to the future only for its restoration.

"There is one institution and one institution alone which is capable of supplying and enforcing the social ethic that is needed to revivify the world. It is an institution at once intranational and international—an institution that can claim to pronounce infallibly on moral matters, and to enforce the observance of its moral decrees by direct sanctions on the individual conscience of men—an institution which, while respecting and supporting the civil government of nations, can claim to exist independently of them, and can insist that they shall not intrude upon the moral life of their citizens." (p179.)

These are the words of the political economist of Southern capitalism in the Home Rule/Sinn Fein/De Valera period. He was not an eccentric. He was a very representative man of his class. That class saw its international significance as a mission to restore the Catholic unity of the world. It was developing capitalism under a feudal ideology. It saturated its own society with this ideology, so that even socialist developments tended to take on a feudal form. In the thirties, Sinn Fein 'socialism' based itself on pronouncement of the Vatican against usurers' capital. This led to the growth of a corporate state ideology in the late thirties, which remained the main radical ideological tendency until the early sixties.

The dominant form of ideology of modern Catholic bourgeois Ireland, resulting from its economic origin in the tenant-farmer movement of the second part of the 19th century, combined with the general guidance of the Catholic Church, has been a kind of mediaevalist Populism.

The South, 1800-1850

The population of Ireland doubled (from 4 to 8 million) between 1760 and 1840. The increase in population in the South was based on a growth of tillage farming in response to increased demand in Britain (due to industrialisation combined with the American and European wars, which occupied most of the period from 1778 to 1815).

This development is comprehensively described by Raymond Crotty in his book, **Irish Agricultural Production** (1966). He shows that Ireland, which had been "a heavy corn importer" around 1760, was a "substantial net exporter of corn" by 1800. From 1660 to 1760 Irish agricultural development was through dairy farming, and, being livestock based, was necessarily slow. This held the increase of population in check. Population growth per annum between 1687 and 1767 was 0.25% (p29).

After the 1770s, population growth was 2.0% per annum. This reflected the change from dairy-farming to tillage. Young men with little or no capital could set up families on smallholdings, growing potatoes to live and corn for the rent. "With the exception of the new countries of North American and Australia in the 19th century, it is difficult if not impossible to find a parallel in rural societies for the exceptional facilities afforded to young people without capital to marry in Ireland in the late 18th and early 19th centuries" (p57). The rapid increase in population increased competition for land, drove up the rents, and "provided the fortunes and confidence to build Ireland's numerous Georgian country mansions and the beautiful Georgian squares and rows in the city of Dublin" (p34).

Wartime prices for corn came to an end with the war in 1815. Agricultural prices as a whole fell, but tillage prices fell more than the prices of grassland products and the latter were stabilised sooner. European corn began to come to Britain again (though the tariffs against it were not abolished till 1848). The British market had been opened to Irish live cattle in the late 18th century, and the cattle prices suffered less than any others. In addition to which, Ireland was more suited by natural conditions to livestock and dairy farming than to tillage. In the new conditions, livestock farming, which is the least labour intensive, became the most profitable.

After 1815, economic forces gave rise to a tendency away from tillage and back to grassland farming. The momentum of tillage and population increase carried through for a long time afterwards. Even the thirty years between Waterloo and the Famine was not long enough to bring it to a halt. The population continued to build up on the basis of habits that no longer had an economic justification.

Southern Irish society was particularly inflexible. It had no stable ruling class, grounded in production, capable of guiding the society. The landlords were an economically useless class of gentlemen, who tended to do less damage when they were absentee than when they were resident. They built their genteel Georgian superstructure on top of the squalid system of rack-rent. (They could not have differed more from the class of capitalist farmers in Britain, who were also known as gentry. Only the name was the same.)

The rack-rented peasantry had not been socially developed in the period of intensive tillage production. But in that period it had been possible for them to marry early on the reasonable expectation of security on the basis of rack-rent. When a thriving rack-rent system on the basis of tillage was no longer possible, old habits continued. Relative to the pattern of demand, there was an immense surplus population on the land, and it continued to grow.

The change from tillage to grassland farming required a fall in the agricultural population, but that population continued to increase. The landlords took few effective measures towards diminishing it. They may have been rack-renters, but they were also genteel. They were not ruthless capitalists, but general rack-renters, and there is a world of difference between the two. As Crotty puts it:

"Perhaps the most important factor of all in permitting the accumulation of an economically excess population on the land was the character of the landlords. These were no self-made captains of industry whose single-minded pursuit of economic gain had brought them to the top. Instead, they were for the most part descendants of the captains and adventurers of two or more centuries earlier who had won the land from the native occupiers. By the 19th century the landlords of Ireland, the descendants of ruthless appropriators, had mellowed and in character were probably no different from ordinary men... Indeed, the life of gracious indolence led by the many absentee landlords, away from the scene where their incomes originated, perhaps made them more easy going as a whole than most other classes of men." (p46.)

Among the factors maintaining an uneconomically high agricultural population on the basis of tillage, and hindering the development of grassland farming, Crotty cites:

"the inability or loathness of landlords for a variety of reasons to clear people from potential pasture land to the extent that purely financial considerations would have warranted" (p46). "One indication of the extent to which landlords fell short of the clearance of people which their economic self interest warranted was the economically surplus population which remained on the land at the outbreak of the Famine... some 20% of the total agricultural population." (p60.)

If the landlords after 1815 had behaved as an agricultural capitalist class, and, using the rate of profit as their golden thread, had applied themselves rigorously to the development of pasture farming, taking all necessary measures to clear away the surplus population left over from the tillage era, they would have gained for themselves a substantial place in the future of Irish society. (Inhumanitarian behaviour, with a sound economic purpose to it, has never failed to find historical justification.)

It was not because they were inhumanitarian, but because they served no economic purpose, that the Anglo-Irish landlords were doomed to economic extinction in the second half of the 19th century.

The problem in Irish agriculture in the first seventy years after the Union was to find the capitalist class. From the Union to the Famine, the Government backed the landlords with the full force of the law, and did everything necessary to facilitate evictions etc. They seem to have mistaken the Anglo-Irish gentry as being of a kind with the British gentry. But the Anglo-Irish gentry failed miserably to become the Irish agricultural capitalist class. The Government recognised this in the 1840s, and availed of the Famine to bankrupt the old gentry and force them to sell their estates. From 1848 to 1870, it was hoped that the new commercial class of landlords would develop capitalist farming, but they too failed.

The middlemen too failed to become the capitalists. And capitalist development among the larger tenant farmers proceeded very slowly until the Famine.

Rural society in the South from the Union to the Famine was made up of an absurdly genteel, and economically ineffective class of rack-rent landlords, a rack-rented peasantry living on a tillage industry which was no longer soundly based, with middlemen, usurers, and parasites of all sorts and descriptions in between. The growth of pasture farming, and of a capitalist tenant-farmer class based on it, was obstructed by the density of population on the land and the genteel character of the landlords.

(During a tour of Ireland in 1856 Engels wrote to Marx: "They have been artificially forced by consistent oppression to become a lumpenised nation... This lumpen characteristic is found in the aristocracy as well. The estate owners, who everywhere else have taken on bourgeois qualities, have become lumpenised here". That is the translation made by Angela Clifford for the B&ICO and given in Engels' **History Of Ireland**, p4. In the collection of Marx/Engels writings, On Ireland, published by the British revisionists in 1971, when the revisionists had become the tail-end of Catholic nationalism in Irish politics, there is a little white lie. The word, *"lumpenised"* in the foregoing letter is translated as "impoverished". But the word is lumpenised; and lumpenised does not mean impoverished; and lumpenised is an apt description. Catholic bourgeois Ireland was beginning to emerge on the basis of the class struggle of the tenant farmers, but the old system still gave the society its atmosphere. The 'tact' of the revisionist intelligentsia responsible for this falsification is entirely misplaced. The Catholic farmers know very well that Catholic Ireland, when it was dominated by an economically useless gentry, was a degraded society. They glory in the fact that they were the class who pulled it out of the lumpen swamp.)

Crotty's historical analysis is remarkably free from nationalist moralising. But, in the following argument, he tends towards moralising of another kind:

"it could be argued with some reason that the payment of high rents by farmers actually tended to relieve destitution before the Famine. In so far as rents reduced the incomes of farmers it made saving and investment more difficult. Investment by farmers at this time and for many years after was practically synonymous with an increase in cattle and sheep stocks. The more cattle and sheep numbers were increased, the greater was the pressure to extend pasture, to reduce tillage and to reduce employment opportunities. In other words, investment was of a labour-replacing nature and because high rents may have slowed down investment they may well have assisted in maintaining the demand for labour and, to that extent, improved rather than worsened the conditions of the poorer classes." (p53.)

"Market conditions, rather than the tenure system, were orientating agriculture away from tillage and towards pastoral farming. Indeed, in so far as the tenure system had any impact on agricultural adjustment, it is possible that through high rents and the effect of these on the ability to save and invest in cattle and sheep, the tenure system slowed down the trend away from tillage and to that extent relieved rather than exacerbated the conditions of the capital-less labouring class." (p55.)

But the point is that, having failed to become the agricultural capitalist class themselves, the landlords through rack-rents obstructed the evolution of a capitalist class from the tenantry. This may have relieved the condition of the mass of the people on the land for a time. But, by permitting the growth of the rural population in such circumstances, it only contributed to a major catastrophe in the long run.

Fintan Lalor—The Prophet of Southern Capitalism In the writings of James Fintan Lalor in the 1840s, the authentic voice of the small commodity producer is heard for the first time in Catholic Ireland. Lalor's writings are suffused with the conviction that the small commodity producer is the source of everything good and useful that is destined to happen in Ireland. Though he wrote in the midst of the Famine, when the peasantry were dying like flies, and were the object of the finer feelings of upper class philanthropists throughout Europe, the tone of his writings is one of scorn for all philanthropic schemes for the betterment of Ireland. While the upper classes were writing laments for the Irish peasantry, that peasantry, in the period of its greatest misery, expressed through Lalor nothing but confidence in itself.

"...the cultivated soil of Ireland is distributed... into about 880,000 landholdings, each occupied by a family. Of these number of landholders, 510,000 were in occupation, each of farms varying in size from one acre to ten... this class of men differed little in appearance; but very much in reality of circumstances and condition from the class of mere labourers... Their means of subsistence were somewhat greater, their securities for subsistence were far greater. They did not, as the labourers did, commonly starve or suffer hunger through the summer times... the *famine months* as we call them. Those of them who held farms of some 5 to 10 acres of holding enjoyed some little share of the comfort of life, which with the careless and slothful temperment of Ireland heightened into happiness. The men dressed well on Sunday, and the women gaily. The smallest landholders of this class were labourers also... labourers with allotments... labourers with assurance against positive starvation. Each man had at least a foothold in existence. Their country had hope for them too, while she had none for the labourer...

"Two circumstances of this man's situation... remain yet to be stated. One of them, is, that he held his land by no other assurance, legal or moral, than his landlord's pecuniary interest in retaining him as a tenant. He had commonly no lease of his holding, or, if he had it was rendered null in effect by numberless circumstances. The feelings that exist in England between landlord and tenant... a feeling of family attachment, the habit of the house, the fashion of the land, the custom of the country; all those things that stand for laws and are stronger than laws... are here unknown. But the working farmer of Ireland who held his own plough, and acted as his own labourer, was able to pay a higher rent for his land than the farmer of any other class; and hence alone he continued to hold it. This was his title of tenure... his only title; his security against the grazing and against the extensive tillage farms; his sole security for leave to live.

"Such is the first circumstance requiring note. The second is this... The occupier I speak of, if his holding was very small put the entire of it in tillage; if large he put a portion into pasture. In either case his tillage ground was appropriated through two crops... a potato crop and a grain crop. He sowed grain for his landlord, he planted potatoes for himself. The corn paid the rent, the potato fed the tenant. When the holding was small, the grain was insufficient, alone, to balance rent; a portion of potatoes made up the deficiency by feeding a hog. When the holding was larger, the grain crop was more than sufficient with the help of a hog, to clear the rent and tithe rent, and country rent and poor rate. In such cases the cultivator had a small surplus, which he could actually dispose of as he liked, and he commonly laid it out in the purchase of mere luxuries, such as shoes, wearing apparel, and other articles of convenience. So stood the landholders of ten acres and under" **(Tenant Right And Landlord Law)**.

At the time of the Famine, the larger tenants had already begun to trade in agricultural produce on their own account, and some had already developed, in fact, to the position of being small capitalist farmers. And the tenant farmer class as a whole was on the verge of entering into trading activity as small commodity farmers. The Famine precipitated the development of this semi-feudal peasantry into a class of small commodity producers, who were the basis of the development of capitalism proper in Southern Ireland. And the manifesto of this new class appeared, appropriately, during the Famine which brought their semi-feudal landlords to bankruptcy.

Lalor dismissed the various administrative schemes being propounded for the development of manufactures. He wrote:

"The agricultural class must precede and provide for every other... Adopt this process; create what has never yet existed in Ireland, an active agricultural peasantry, able to accumulate as well as to produce... do this, and you raise a thriving and happy community, a solid economy, a prosperous people, an effective nation. Create the husbandman, and you create the mechanic, the artisan, the manufacturer, the merchant. All the natural motives and means with which man is endowed will come then to your relief and assistance and do the rest...

"We are in the habit of hearing it asserted that a large development of manufacturing industry is what Ireland needs, and that to establish it should be her chief object. It is assumed, not infrequently, that a manufacturing system must precede, and is the only mode of promoting, the improvement of agriculture itself. This is an error I could wish to see abandoned. I am prepared to prove that neither by the private enterprise of individuals or companies, neither by force of national feeling anyhow exerted, neither by public association or public action of any kind or extent nor by government aid... neither by these or any other means and appliances can a manufacturing system be established in Ireland, nor so much as a factory built on firm ground, until the support of a numerous and efficient agricultural yeomanry be first secured...

"My general object, the formation of a new social economy, thus resolves itself into the formation of a new agricultural system. The principles on which the new system is to be founded must either be settled by agreement between the landowners and the people, or they must be settled by a struggle." (**To The Landowners Of Ireland**, April 19, 1847.)

What effect did the Famine have on the development of the old peasantry into an agricultural yeomanry? It brought about a drastic reduction in the peasantry through starvation and emigration. But there can be no doubt that, in terms of class development, it was the peasantry who benefited from it. The landlords individually did not starve during the famine as did the peasantry. But the Famine brought the old landlord class to ruin, while it speeded up the economic development of, and legal emancipation of, the peasantry. The Famine played a role in Ireland similar to that which the Black Death in the 14th century played in the development of the English serfs into a free peasantry.

Historians are usually misled by consideration of the sufferings of the peasantry during the Famine, and the callousness displayed by the landlord class, into assuming that the landlords benefited from it; that it enabled them to intensify the oppression of the peasantry. In fact, it had the contrary effect. It was not a period of worsening, but a period of steadily improving conditions, that followed the Famine. Twenty years after the Famine the tenants became joint owners of their farms; thirty years later they became virtual owners; fifty years later they were in fact and in form the absolute owners.

Through the Encumbered Estates Courts, the Government brought the traditional landlord class to bankruptcy in their hour of need. They were forced to sell their estates to pay their debts. Free trade in land was established at a stroke. Merchants bought up the estates. It seems to have been imagined that this was the institution of capitalist land ownership. But, as Marx pointed out, the intrusion of merchants' capital into any form of production tends to aggravate its worst features. It cannot in itself bring about the organisation of capitalist production. The new commercial landlords of Southern Ireland disrupted whatever tenuous good feeling had been built up between the old landlord class and the tenants, but were in no respect any more successful than the old. And they faced a tenantry which had undergone considerable class development in a very brief period. The British ruling class soon came to realise that the agricultural capitalist class of Southern Ireland was still latent in the peasantry, and that the new commercial landlords were no more useful economically than the genteel landlords. Parliament had guaranteed the new landlords absolute ownership of the land in 1849. In 1870, it reduced them to part owners with their tenants, recognising that this was the fact of the matter.

The Famine speeded up the development of the peasantry by cutting down on its large cottier element. It thereby relieved the intense competition for land which hitherto had obstructed class development. Coherent class struggle, of a kind which had developed a century previously in Ulster, was begun with remarkable speed by the peasantry after the Famine. The Tenant Leagues of 1850 were a qualitatively new social phenomenon in the South.

On the psychological level, the Famine accomplished in a lesser degree what had been accomplished by the Reformation struggles in England and Scotland. Descriptions of the Catholic peasantry before the Famine all stress their laziness, drunkenness and frivolity. There was little point in their being otherwise. Thrift was no virtue in the rack-rent system. The whole system encouraged the small peasant to behold the lilies in the field, who did not sow, neither did they reap. The parable of the talents had no relevance to them. Arthur Young describes them thus:

"Lazy to an extent at *work*, but so spiritually active at *play*, that at *hurling*, which is the cricket of savages, they show the greatest feats of agility." (Volume 2, p147.)

The shock given by the Famine brought about a profound change in behaviour, and developed new habits of a more cautious and calculating kind, at the precise moment when changing economic conditions made such habits advantageous. It is frequently said that the Famine turned Irish Catholicism towards Jansenism. (Jansenism was a Puritan development within Catholicism in France in the 18th century, in response to bourgeois social development.)

[Some years after this was written, I realised that "Jansenism" was a very misleading misnomer for the new religious development in Catholic Ireland, which began around the middle of the 19th century. I have gone into this in **The Dubliner: The Lives, Times And Writings Of James Clarence Mangan**, (Athol Books, 1988). What it had in common with Jansenism was strictness of behaviour. The comparison therefore holds up well enough in economic, though not in religious, conduct. BC. Note to 1992 Edition.]

Crotty maintains that "the Great Famine was not a true watershed in Irish social and economic history; rather the change in demand conditions on the British market which was heralded by the Battle of Waterloo represented such a watershed" (p64). But that depends on which is meant by "watershed". The change in demand after 1815 was prevented by counter-acting causes from effecting extensive economic and social changes for thirty years. Crotty points out that a tendency towards pasture farming set in soon after Waterloo, that the rate of growth of the population had gradually been reduced, and that the expansion of tillage had slowly been halted. But, prior to the Famine, these developments were marginal. The requisite changes which failed to occur in a controlled way in the period immediately after Waterloo, occurred in a catastrophic way thirty years later.

The old landlord class on top of a society was bankrupted. The large surplus population based on tillage at the bottom of society was drastically reduced by starvation and emigration. Suddenly, the more substantial tenant farmers, based on grassland farming, developed into a coherent and powerful class. The period of organised and powerful tenant-right struggle set in immediately in 1850. The sharp agrarian conflict of the following years was not caused by an intensification of landlord oppression, but by an increase in the power and aspirations of the peasantry. The tenant-farmers had become a coherent class, asserting rights for themselves on the land. Once that happened, laws became powerless to guarantee the landlord interest.

Legal fetishism in history is thoroughly exposed in periods like this. Laws are effective which are based on a real balance of class and economic forces. When landlordism was triumphant, it was not basically because it had legal backing. And when the tenant-right movement established itself as the most powerful social force in Southern Ireland after 1850, it was not because the law had been changed. Landlordism was no less supported by law after 1850 than before. In fact, landlord ownership was made legally more absolute, and the legal right to evict was more clearly established, in the 1850s than in the earlier period, in an attempt to give the new commercial landlord class a good start. But legislation was no more able to consolidate effective landlord ownership in the South after 1850, than it had been in the North in the 18th century. And within twenty years the law was changed to accord with the new reality.

Appendix

"Men Of No Property"? It is not often that one comes across Marxists who conceive of the struggle to establish bourgeois property rights as a struggle which is in conflict with the "men of property". But, in the British 'left' romances about Ireland, notions are propounded, which would be considered self-evidently absurd in any other context. So it is with International Socialism, in its pamphlet, **Ireland's History Of Oppression**, where we read:

> "The Land war had been the biggest mass movement in Ireland since the tithe war but its leaders were closely involved with the parliamentary Home Rule party, which was dominated by Irish property owners. It was once again demonstrated that 'the men of property' would always compromise when matters reached an extreme. Parnell agreed to call off the land war in return for the release of all prisoners and state payment of arrears of rent."

The tenant-farmers—who were by this time powerfully developing bourgeois property owners—are here conceived of as "men of no property", betrayed by the "men of property" of the Home Rule Party. The land war was a conflict between two classes of "men of property"—a thoroughly bourgeois class (the tenant farmers), and a semi-feudal remnant (the landlords).

Partition

Catholic Nationalism The economic development of the South subsequent to the land reform is relatively well known and need not be dealt with here. But a few observations need to be made on the national character of the Catholic nation that was forged in the 19th century. The revolution in land ownership that was accomplished in the last quarter of the 19th century was thorough, and was far-reaching in its social and political effects. As Connolly observed:

> "The Land Acts dispossessed the landlords and thus ended the economic influence on which their political power is based. Hence outside Ulster, the landed aristocracy ceased to be a power in politics. An agricultural labourer would have a greater chance to be elected than a landlord in the South-West and east of Ireland would have by his former tenants." (**Forward**, August 16, 1913.)

Furthermore:

> "It is interesting to observe how Ireland has been and is being made the scene of many radical experiments in legislation which, in any other country, would only be looked for as the result of a great Socialist upheaval." (Ibid.)

The thoroughness and speed of the revolution in land ownership was the result not merely of the tenant struggles, but of the combined actions of the tenant struggles and the state. The British state became ever more bourgeois and radical in the course of the 19th century, and in consequence became ever less sympathetic to the Southern Irish landlords. When this powerful industrial capitalist state decided that the time had come when the Irish landlords should cease to exist as an economic class, there was little that the landlords could do about it. While the British state did not create the new economic situation—and while the land reform legislation only served the development of, and was not the source of, the increasing economic power of the tenant farmer class—it is is nevertheless the case that the British state superstructure served the development of the new, popular, capitalist economic forces in Irish agriculture with remarkable efficiency. And this exercise of the power of the British industrial capitalist class undoubtedly contributed to the grossly exaggerated view which developed in Catholic nationalist Ireland of the power of legislation to determine economic development.

By contrast with this, there prevailed in industrial Ulster a very sober estimate of the economic power of legislation. It was well realised that, while intelligent commercial legislation can facilitate economic development, it cannot create it. The economic development of Ulster had made its way for a very long time against unfavourable legislation, and this fact reflected itself in the national psychology of the Ulster Protestant community. When the conflict of the two communities over Home Rule was launched in the 1880s, the lack of economic realism and the Utopian view of the power of legislation, which prevailed in the Catholic nationalist movement, were large factors in making the Ulster industrialists determined that their industries should not come under Southern administration.

(Engels wrote to Marx on 27th September, 1869: "The worst thing about the Irish is that they become corruptible as soon as they cease being peasants and become bourgeois. Admittedly this is the case with all peasant nations. But it is especially bad in Ireland." The farmers were the backbone of Catholic bourgeois Ireland. In the other sections of the rising bourgeoisie there was a strong atmosphere of confidence trickery. It is appropriate that the most substantial and objective economic history so far to be produced in Catholic bourgeois Ireland—Crotty's—should come from an agricultural economist.)

The dominant ideology of Southern nationalist politics changed considerably in the course of the 19th century. O'Connell, the founder of the Catholic nationalist movement, brought a combination of Whiggery and liberal Catholicism to it. O'Connell came from a Catholic landowning background, and was in the forefront of the Catholic middle class development in the British legal profession. But the mass of the people in his movement were the politically and ideologically inert subjects of political manipulation. O'Connell was a Whig "King of the beggars". If O'Connell took his social ideas from the Whig bourgeois aristocracy, those ideas had little relevance to his followers.

[It says here that O'Connell "brought a combination of Whiggery and liberal Catholicism" to the nationalist movement. I have not looked at this publication since I wrote it twenty years ago, and I am astonished to find this statement in it. Maybe it is what I wrote, though I think I knew twenty years ago that O'Connell kept pace with the Ultramontanist religious development. Or maybe something happened in the typing. Anyhow, an accurate statement would be: "O'Connell brought a combination of Whiggery, economic liberalism and Romanist Catholicism to the nationalist movement". In his economic ideology he was an arid Benthamite liberal. BC. Note to 1992 edition.]

The "beggars" gave rise to a strong tenant-farmer class in the second part of the 19th century, and eventually to a powerful class of farmer owners in the early twentieth century. After O'Connell, the Nationalist movement went through a period of Ascendancy leadership under G.H. Moore, Isaac Butt, and finally,

Parnell. Elements in Anglo-Ireland conceived of the Ascendancy as the catalyst, which would bring the Catholic and Ulster Protestant communities together, and give the resulting nation a moderate bourgeois liberal ideology. But, after the overthrow of Parnell, Catholic Ireland began to come into its own politically.

Connolly once said that the workers should do what the farmers had done since the latter part of the 19th century—compel society to accept the standard of their class interest as the only true social standard. The workers have still not done that (and, in fact, soon after Connolly made that remark, it was the workers who were compelled to accept the world outlook of the farmers). The farmers, first as tenants, later as joint owners, and finally as absolute owners, grew uninterruptedly in economic, political and general social power for a century after 1850. Their economic interest, their political interest and their general world outlook became predominant in society.

The politics and ideology prevailing in the 1850s, whether of the Ascendancy, or Catholic merchant or professional class, were all made obsolete in the next eighty years. Parnell may have had it in mind to 'use' the tenant farmers to give substance to a kind of national movement which would include Anglo-Ireland in a leading position. In the event, it was Parnell who was used until such time as the forces being generated by the tenant-farmers could take their politics into their own hands. Parnell's party machine was taken over by the priests, on behalf of the farmers. And when Tim Healy eventually challenged Parnell's leadership of the party over the issue of divorce, and, in reply to Parnell's statement that he was master of the party, asked his celebrated question, "Ah, but who is mistress of the party?", he was a portent of things to come. Anglo-Ireland continued to hold considerable property, but, after the fall of Parnell, its political influence was negligible. Parnell's most vigorous lieutenants were Catholic lawyers or journalists. After his overthrow, the Parnellite position was reduced to a small faction led by Redmond, a large Catholic landowner. But outside the Redmondite faction there was a continuous grading into Sinn Fein.

The politicians of the Catholic middle class at first came mostly from the legal profession, with journalism later being added. When the Party was organised, the category of professional politician made its appearance. This Catholic intelligentsia of the Party came to be regarded in the Sinn Fein period as having been corrupted by the peculiar kind of political activity in which it was engaged in at Westminster. But more than corruption happened to the Party members in London. The fact that they spent much of their time in Westminster agitating on a single issue, and that they were not at all involved in the administration of Ireland, certainly had a corrupting influence on them. But it also had a liberalising effect on them ideologically. Eventually, many of them were saved both from corruption and from liberalism by the development in Ireland of a political movement which refused to go to Westminster, and which was responding to the new economic developments taking place in Ireland. In Sinn Fein—and its derivative organisations, Fianna Fail and Fine Gael—the social development, which was taking place on the basis of the achievements of the farmers, came into its own politically and ideologically. (Sinn Fein will be used here as a term embracing the original Sinn Fein and Fianna Fail and Fine Gael, as well as the present Sinn Fein rump.)

Through the development of Sinn Fein, Catholic Ireland was forged into a strong national movement which (by comparison with what had ever existed previously in Catholic Ireland) was exceptionally self-reliant and democratic. But the very process, which developed this strong national movement among Catholics, cut it off from the Protestants. The general culture of the movement drew lines of national demarcation between Catholic Ireland and the rest of Ireland and Britain. The culture of the Ulster Protestant community came within the category, "foreign". The Gaelic Athletic Association (which was a focal point of nationalist political development in the late 19th and early 20th centuries) declared the games traditionally played by the Catholic community to be national, and other games to be foreign. And members of the GAA were prohibited from playing, or even watching, these "foreign" games—which were played in Protestant Ulster. Similarly, the Gaelic League designated certain dances as national, and others as foreign and anti-national.

These games and dances were not simply peculiar to the Catholic community, but were appropriate to a peasant rather than an industrial society. There were therefore two grounds which would have prevented them from appealing to the large industrial proletariat in the North.

A third great element in this national culture was Gaelic language revivalism. The nationalist aim of reviving Gaelic as the language of the nation could make a strong appeal in the South, where the greater part of the population had been Gaelic-speaking as late as the 1840s. But the Ulster Protestant community, which had never been a Gaelic speaking community, merely viewed it as a threat to impose an alien language on them.

Fourthly, there was the Catholic religion. The national movement in the South was decisively Catholic, and the state which it eventually constructed was a Catholic state. The Republican movement, which has recently been flirting with secularism, has been attempting to represent the dominance achieved by the Catholic Church in the South as something which was *imposed* by some outside, or "anti-national", force on the society, and as therefore being somehow unreal. In fact, Catholicism was very much part of the reality of the national movement, and the dominance of the Church was far from having been imposed from above.

The Catholic Church, the greatest persecuting and martyring force in the history of Europe, likes to propagate among its members an image of itself as a persecuted and martyred assembly. It is only in Ireland that this image had any reality. It is only in Ireland that it was the Church of the dispossessed. And, when the dispossessed of the 18th century came into their own as farmers of the late 19th and 20th century, they brought that Church to general social and political dominance.

Italy, Spain and Ireland are often bracketed together as Catholic countries, but there are a number of substantial differences between the position of the Catholic Church in Ireland and its position in Spain or Italy. In the first place, its power is far greater in Ireland than in Italy or Spain. In the latter countries, substantial popular movements have arisen within the national society against the Church, and at particular moments have gained political supremacy over it. The national democracy of Italy rose in arms against the Church in the mid-19th century and drove the Pope into exile. For a long period subsequently he was the prisoner in the Vatican. The position of the Vatican was relieved by the rise of Italian fascism. In Spain, likewise, there was a popular movement against the Church, from which the Church was saved by the Spanish fascists. But in Ireland the power of the Church has never been seriously threatened from within Catholic society. And the Church rose to supremacy, not in defiance of, but through the rise of, the national democracy.

What Marx said of the Heavenly Kingdom Rebellion in China in the mid 19th century can be applied to the Catholic nationalist movement in Ireland:

> "...this is a war *pro aris et focis* [i.e. for the altar and the hearth], a popular war for the maintenance of Chinese nationality, with all its overbearing

prejudice, stupidity, learned ignorance and pedantic barbarism if you like, but yet a popular war" **(New York Tribune,** June 5, 1857).

It is as false to deny that Catholicism in Ireland was popular, as that the national movement was Catholic. The reactionary Catholic Church was popularly based in Ireland and was carried to supremacy by a popular revolution. To deny that originality of the Irish situation is to be incapable of understanding the Irish situation historically.

But, while it must be insisted that Catholicism was a popular force in part of Ireland, and that the Church rose through the action of popular forces to a kind of supremacy in comparison with which the alleged supremacy of the Orange Order in Northern Ireland is a pale shadow, it must also be insisted that it remained the Catholic Church—reactionary in its ideology, intolerant in its outlook, and committed to social legislation on the basis of its theology.

It was the very fact that the Catholic Church was rising to supremacy through the action of popular forces that generated such apprehension in Ulster. If the Church had been under the control of some developed bourgeois political forces in the South, and if it could have been said that these forces were 'using' the Church, an accommodation between Ulster and the South might, in this sphere, have been a possibility. The religious tolerance of some of the Redmondites is sometimes pointed out in this connection. But the liberalism that might have rubbed off on some members of the Irish Party in London had little relevance in Ireland. It was clearly realised in Ulster that the Party did not control the Bishops, that the position of the Party was being threatened by more popular forces, that these more popular forces were even more Catholic than the Party, and that therefore any guarantees given by the Party in connection with the position of Ulster under an all-Ireland Government wouldn't be worth the paper they were written on—even assuming the Party's intentions to be honourable, which was a big assumption.

The Industrialisation Of Ulster The rapid industrialisation of Ulster has been the subject of a great amount of Catholic nationalist apologetics of the kind which has been so often quoted already in this book. The purpose of much of these apologetics is to obscure either the actual fact of the contradictory economic developments which took place in North and South, or the causes of those contradictory developments, or both. At times, this amounts to actual fetishism: to a conviction that, if theoretical models can be constructed in which the contradictory economic developments are not represented, the developments which actually took place can be conjured out of the actual history of Ireland. Of course, the only effect of that approach is to make a complete mystery of the political situation which has existed since 1886. Historical development which has actually taken place can be denied in fantasy, but one is still left with the actual consequences of that historical development. And, since the actual historical causes of the existing situation are denied in fantasy, a fantasy history must be made up to account for the existing situation. Hence we find people who are supposed to be materialists attributing supernatural powers to the Orange Order.

Cullen, in his Economic History, having depicted the linen industry in the late 18th century as being "far flung in the island", and as being popularly based in the South (and then mentioning the Southern industry no more) proceeds to give the same treatment to engineering and shipbuilding in the 19th century. He writes:

"Between 1831 and 1931 the number of male shipwrights doubled, male glassworkers rose by 50%, ironfounders by 25%, ropeworkers by 20%. Nor was this activity in any way centred on Ulster. In shipbuilding, 40% of the shipwrights were in Munster in 1841, reflecting the rapidly expanding shipbuilding industries of Cork and Waterford. The yards in both centres were the most enterprising in Ireland; the first paddle steamer made in Ireland was built in Cork in 1812, and the Cork and Waterford yards were pioneers in the 1840s of iron shipbuilding in Ireland. Less than a third of the ironfounders were in the north. The ironworks in Dublin and Cork were very active. There were two manufacturers of steam engines in Dublin, four in Cork, and at least two in Belfast... A famous firm which made locomotives was still open in Drogheda. In one regard, however, Belfast was beginning to emerge as leader—in a miscellaneous category called 'machine workers' of whom 60% were in Ulster in 1841. They probably made miscellaneous goods, especially textile machinery." (p124.)

Cullen makes no attempt to deal with the dynamics of the situation, and makes no attempt to explain the internal causes of the developments which took place during the succeeding half-century.

The fact that a vigorous industrial capitalist society was developing in Ulster did not mean that, at a given moment, there was more large scale industry in Ulster than in the South. Eventually, of course, this became so. At the beginning of the 19th century, the healthy nucleus of an industrial capitalist society existed in Ulster. In the South, the healthy nucleus did not exist, though a number of industries did exist as more or less extraneous elements.

The following description of the development of the engineering and shipbuilding in Ulster in the 19th century is taken from **The Engineering Industry Of The North Of Ireland** (by W.E. Coe, 1969):

"Throughout the 19th century Dublin was a more important ironfounding centre than Belfast, and in the first half of the century had twice as many foundries as Belfast." (p24.)

"Belfast was not the place where steamships were first constructed in Ireland. The first steamer built in Ireland appears to have been the *City of Cork*, completed by Andrew and Michael Hennessy of Passage in 1816... In 1817 they built the *Waterloo*, and the engines on this occasion were made in Cork; this was claimed to be the first steamship completely fitted out in Ireland. In the first half of the 19th century Cork was a much more important shipbuilding centre than Belfast" (p78.)

Ships were also built in Dublin, Drogheda and Waterford.

"the first iron vessel launched in Belfast was constructed, not in one of the existing shipbuilding yards, but by the engineering and boilermaking firm of Victor Coates and Co. This was the *Countess of Caledon*, an iron steamer of 30 h.p. launched in 1838" (p78).

"It was not until 1853 that a second firm undertook iron shipbuilding on the Lagan; in that year the Belfast Harbour Commissioners laid out a yard on the Queen's Island for Robert Hickson, a partner in the Eliza St. ironworks in Belfast, but the yard did not begin to prosper until it was taken over by Hickson's manager, E.J. Harland, in 1858... [In] 1868 MacIlwaine and Lewis began ship repairing at the Abercorn Basin, and the 1870s branched out into shipbuilding. Later, in 1880, the other form of Belfast shipbuilders, Workman Clark and Co., laid out their first keel" (p78).

"Few of the early engineering works in the north of Ireland were established by local men: Job Rider, John Hind, Stephen Cotten, George

Honer, and E.J.H. Harland came from England, James Combe and James Mackie from Scotland. From the middle of the 19th century, however, local main trained in the original works began to set up in business for themselves or to take over the management of existing firms when the founders retired or got into financial difficulties" (p193).

"The men who created the engineering industry were practical engineers; even in the relatively prosperous North of Ireland the landowners did nothing to help the development of engineering, and little assistance was forthcoming from the linen or other local industries. Those who became partners in the early engineering works, without themselves being engineers, were few in number and had little in common. When Victor Coates joined the firm which owned the Lagan Foundry, he was a hairdresser in Castle St., and he continued taking orders for the foundry at his hairdressing establishment until, on the death of Edward Stainton, he found himself in control of the business... In contrast with many enterprises which failed in the south because they were set up by men with capital but no business experience, the engineering firms in the north of Ireland were started by practical engineers, backed in some cases by local men with business experience as well as wealth." (p194.)

In the Harland and Wolff partnership: "Harland was the inventive genius, Wolff the financier, Wilson the practical naval architect, and Pirrie the businessman and salesman, but all were able engineers who could, and did, undertake each others' work when necessary." (p197.)

In 1844, an economist who was as much abreast of the times as R.R. Kane wrote:

"The causes which had led to the bad results of the manufacturing system in the sister kingdom, do not exist with us. Ireland cannot become a great manufacturing country, such as England is. Her physical constitution does not supply materials. The proportion of her people employed in factories can, therefore, never be so great. Her sources of power, whether it be coal or turf, or water, lie distributed so uniformly through the land, that the concentration of manufacturers, on a few localities, as in England, cannot occur." (Industrial Resources, p426.)

This was written on the eve of the great development of heavy industry in Belfast.

Anti-partitionists point to the extensive participation of British capitalists in the development of the engineering and shipbuilding industries of Ulster, and seem to imagine that this somehow diminishes the reality of those industries. But British capital came so readily to Ulster, and was so successful there, only because capitalism was developing vigorously in Ulster as part of the British market. British capitalists came into an area of strongly developing capitalism and contributed to that development, and local capitalists strengthened themselves out of this further development. Only a petty-bourgois nationalist would moralise about such a thing. It is a normal feature of the development of capitalism.

In the growth of large-scale industrial capitalism in Ulster in the latter half of the 19th century, the Ulster economy became irretrievably part of the British economy. And this development took place during the very decades when the land reform was creating a popular base for the development of small scale capitalists in the South, who aspired to protect their home market against British competition.

Home Rule And Unionism In 1886 the two communities in Ireland, whose economic history has been described here, were in every sphere of their activity moving strongly in opposite directions. In one, a strong national separatist movement was developing: the other was in process of merging nationally with Britain. In one, an economic policy of national protectionism was being demanded in order to foster the growth of its weak manufactures: in the other the maintenance of free trade relations with the British market was required to serve its large scale industries. In one, grossly exaggerated notions of the power of economic policy prevailed; in the other, there was a hard headed economic realism. The national culture developed by the nationalist movement of the Catholic community reflected exclusively the history, traditions, customs aspirations, and general outlook and values of the Catholic community, and had the effect of repelling, rather than attracting, the masses of the Protestant community. The national movement in the South was obviously bringing the Catholic Church to social supremacy, and the unique phenomenon occurred of a popular bourgeois national movement which equated liberty and Catholicism. Ulster (reflecting in its own history the general history of the struggle for democracy in Europe), saw liberty existing in inverse proportion to the influence of the Catholic Church.

When in 1886 the British Government proposed to place Ulster under a Southern Irish Government, a powerful popular movement arose in Ulster to prevent this proposal from ever becoming a reality. The industrial working class, the farmers, the urban bourgeoisie and petty bourgeoisie, and a landlord element, constituted this movement. Thirty-five years later, the formal political partition took place (inevitably leaving national minorities on either side). It did not take place because the British ruling class brought it about. The scheming of the British ruling class was on the whole directed towards the working out of a compromise between the two communities in Ireland, which would make it possible to establish an all Ireland political structure, which would have served British policy towards Ireland much better than partition.

The British bourgeoisie was not unduly concerned about Irish protectionism. It realised the severe limits to what protectionism could achieve in Ireland. Many of its politicians saw Irish protectionism as a phase of development to be got over as quickly as possible. They had no real fears that the Irish economy would take off on its own and move farther and farther apart from the British economy as time passed. After the limits of protectionist policies had been demonstrated in practice, they expected a voluntary movement back towards integration with Britain. (As one British propagandist put it in 1886, in a Biblical quote: "And Pharaoh said, I will let you; only you will not go very far away." Exodus, VII, 28.)

The notion that British capitalism needed to partition Ireland in order to retain its economic connections with it, and its political influence in it, has little or no relation to historical reality. In fact, it is Partition that has been chiefly responsible for perpetuating strong anti-British feeling in Catholic Ireland since the twenties—and this was an easily predictable consequence of Partition.

But the Ulster bourgeoisie, who would have been *behind* the protective barriers and at the mercy of the Southern administration, could not afford to take a long term view of the matter.

At the time of the second Home Rule Bill (1893) a deputation from the Belfast Chamber of Commerce, the Belfast Harbour Commissioners, and the Belfast Linen Merchants' Association met Gladstone to present their case against Home Rule. Thomas Sinclair, whose great grandfather had drafted United Irish documents, was their spokesman:

"It was an indisputable thing, and beyond the sphere of argument with those who lived in Belfast, that the condition precedent to their progress was their connexion with Great Britain through the legislative Union. That again gave the commercial classes a sense of security as absolute as that which existed in London: and prior to 1886 no Ulster banker or capitalist ever dreamt of being offered a less valuable security for his investment. As an integral part of the United Kingdom they had shared to the full in the commercial legislation in which Mr. Gladstone had borne such an honourable part, and in all the great progress of industry in the great centres of England which followed the loosening of the shackles of trade they had shared. They thought their share was even more remarkable, because while Manchester, Leeds, Nottingham and other towns had coal and iron at their own door, Belfast had not. The mineral resources of Belfast in 1891 were only valued at £400,000, whereas they were almost £100,000,000 in Gt. Britain; and they had so far outgrown their power of producing flax that they imported two-thirds of that staple of their great industry. That expansion was owing to their share in the commercial legislation of Great Britain. In 1861 their population was 100,000; now it was 260,000. Early in the fifties there was not a single iron shipbuilding industry in Belfast. Since that time Englishmen like Sir Edward Harland and Scotchmen like Mr. George Clark felt that they had the same security in Ulster as they had at home, and they came and founded those wonderful ship-building yards which now employed 10,000 or 12,000 male hands. The deputation complained that the security which had caused their progress was going to be taken away and that they were going to have a worse security. In what proportion would their commercial interests be represented in the Legislative Assembly of Dublin? They all knew that Ireland was an agricultural country mainly: they knew that her rural to her urban constituencies were in the relation of about six to one... They therefore said that intricate questions of commercial policy and of commercial matters could not possibly be adequately discussed in a Parliament of that kind, in which the preponderating class was a class which had had no experience in any such measures in the British Parliament... They were being offered for their investments a less security and a lower *status* politically than that which they had at present. With regard to the safeguards which were proposed, he contended that it was a disability to place any citizen of the United Kingdom in a position where he needed a safeguard. No Englishman and no Scotchman at the present moment needed a safeguard, because he was surrounded by a population which was absolutely homogeneous: and they who were citizens of Ireland required at the moment no safeguard because their fortunes were linked with those of the just and generous people of Great Britain. They protested against having to do their business as commercial men under disabilities which were imposed upon no other citizen of the United Kingdom. The great bulk of the manufactures of Belfast and Ulster found their market abroad, so that they were really a business community doing an export business, and they required their civil status to be placed on an equality with the other citizens and manufacturers of the United Kingdom and also with the great centres of industry on the Continent of Europe. What they feared about the Parliament under which they were proposed to be put was that by the imposition of bounties and by the unsettlement of credit which would be caused by the power to alter the franchise within six years, they would be placed at such a disadvantage, compared with their fellow citizens in

England, with whom they were at present on an equality, that they would not be able to compete, and their industries would be destroyed. That was the reason for the fall of prices which was shown in the report [i.e., a fall in stock prices resulting from the Home Rule Bill]; that was the reason why so many of them contemplated removing their industries elsewhere..."

Sinclair concluded:

"A large number of the deputation were old followers of Mr. Gladstone. They had worked hard for the abolition of religious ascendancy, for the establishment of electoral freedom, and for the reform of the land laws, which it was Mr. Gladstone's honour to have given to the country. Would that Mr. Gladstone had allowed those measures to produce their effect and had given them time, and had proceeded as he had in England by giving them a local measure of county government before the desperate measure which was now proposed." (Chamber of Commerce pamphlet, p6-9.)

A Chamber of Commerce Reply to Gladstone, issued on April 11, 1893, says:
"We asked for 'any definite statement of social or material improvements to Ireland likely to result from this Bill'. To this request you made no reply. We pointed out that the only means towards such ends suggested by the Nationalist Party indicate a system of Bounties. This is heresy against Free Trade, but you have not repudiated that programme... You have told us that these men to whom we are opposed preach a doctrine of public plunder, yet you have not offered a shadow of a reason to satisfy us that they will not use their powers, with which you propose to entrust them, to put those doctrines in force." (p22.)

"You next challenge our statement of the existence of mutual historical jealousy in Ireland. We have purposely avoided anything but the most guarded reference to the differences which exist on the religious question. We have not uttered, and shall not utter, a word that could wound the susceptibilities of the Roman Catholics of this country, with whom we all earnestly desire to live on terms of peace and equality. What we did point to is the fact, to which no statesman should be blind, that there is, most unhappily, a line of cleavage which goes deep down into the masses of the people, and by which they are radically divided." (p22.)

From a Report of the Council of the Chamber of Commerce (March 18, 1893):
"We believe that the Economic and Social condition of Ireland renders it singularly unfitted for Home Rule. The population is not homogeneous—it is radically divided on the line of race and religion, and the two parties are filled with distrust and historical jealousy of each other. The chief Economic necessity of the country is the development of manufactures, trade and commerce; but the vast majority of the population have no appreciation of the conditions under which alone such necessities can be met. They do not seem to know that, while a Government can destroy prosperity by destroying security and credit, no Government can create it in the face of insecurity and suspicion." (p40.)

"In Belfast, under the shelter of the Union, protected by British Commercial laws, with the advantage of British Fiscal Legislation in which we share, there has grown up the first really great development of trade and industry ever known in the history of this country. From Belfast, as a centre, business has spread and is spreading. Londonderry, Coleraine, Ballymena, Lisburn, Lurgan, Banbridge, Gilford, Portadown, Cookstown, Strabane, Dungannon, and many other towns are closely connected with Belfast by commercial ties... The development of that trade is entirely dependent on the maintenance of a sense of security; and it is useless to shut our eyes to the fact that the mere introduction of the Bill... has seriously shaken credit. It is notorious... that there has recently been a most marked fall in the best Irish stocks, and that local shares, which sold freely until 13th February, are at present almost unsaleable; and... precisely the same sort of depression was created by the introduction of the Home Rule Bill of 1886. The depreciation of values in Irish securities already amounts to £3,000,000 sterling. We may add that from no political quarter has any assurance been given that this Bill, even if passed, will really secure a final settlement of the Irish question. It would seem therefore that agitation, uncertainty and consequently insecurity are to be perpetuated in Ireland.

"We find no provisions in the Bill calculated to allay these growing apprehensions... The safeguards provided we regard as wholly nominal, and of no practical operative value, and we are confirmed in this view by finding them... treated with derision by the Nationalist press." To the Home Rule Parliament, "trade, manufactures and commerce must appear on sufferance only—in a hopeless minority, unable to protect in the smallest degree the interests of the class." (p42.)

In addition to which, industrial Ulster was at that time greatly under-represented in Parliament relative to the rest of Ireland, and would be under-represented in the Home Rule Parliament. It was to be left up to the Nationalist Party to decide whether Ulster was to be given equal representation:

"The public utterances of the Nationalist leaders, and the many resolutions passed by public meetings and Boards of Guardians in many parts of Ireland, have shown such disregard, not merely of equity between man and man, but of economic principles, that the thought of important powers being devolved on the representatives of such ideas fills us with consternation...

"We have asked in vain for any definite statement of social or material improvement to Ireland likely to result from this Bill. The only methods towards such ends suggested by the Nationalists point to Protection and Bounties; and we note that, while the Bill excludes Protective Duties, there is nothing to prevent an extravagant system of Bounties. It is therefore manifest that the majority are to be at liberty to waste taxes raised in Belfast and Ulster, in an attempt to create and foster trades in other places on a false and unnatural foundation... In addition to the Bounty system, we need only instance here the income tax, the death duties, the transfer of stamp duties, and the licensing system—any one of which can easily be manipulated, under the Bill, against a hostile minority. We conceive we have a right to say we cannot rely upon the character of the Nationalist leaders in dealing with commercial interests" (p45.)

For these various reasons, it is

"beyond question if the Bill passes into law, large amounts of capital, and many branches of industrial enterprise will migrate to Gt. Britain, or the United States or the Colonies."

The Report concludes by emphasising that the economic development of Ulster took place

"under **precisely the same laws as those which govern the other cities and provinces of Ireland**. It is specially noteworthy that the raw material employed in our staple manufactures is chiefly imported... There is no privilege in this respect that is not open to every other city or town in our island." (p46.)

Sinn Fein And Partition Griffith's Sinn Fein was very conscious of its economic mission in the South. It was conscious of itself as the political representative of the budding manufacturing capitalism which required a period of protection for its effective development. (Though it should be noted that Griffith ideologically prefered to speak of the "national system of economy", rather than capitalism, that he shared much of the Catholic mediaevalist ideology of George O'Brien, and that he was far from being immune to economic fads such as "Bimetallism". Nevertheless, he was an unequivocal advocate of industrial development.)

Sinn Fein, therefore, could not admit that the Unionist movement too, in its opposition to Sinn Fein, represented a sound economic interest. It would have been fatal to the morale of the original Sinn Fein to recognise the sound economic basis of Unionism. Griffith was not an economic reactionary—though Sinn Fein subsequently became, and presently is, economically reactionary. The present-day Sinn Fein could cheerfully destroy large scale industry in the name of "anti-imperialism". It can sense the connection between large scale industry and Unionism, and see that connection as a good reason for destroying large-scale industry. ("Economic demolition" is the name given to this activity.)

Griffith was a class conscious bourgeois politician, who had the interests of capitalist industry at heart. Some present-day Sinn Feiners reject him as a bourgeois, but they deviate from capitalism in a mediaevalist or petty bourgeois direction, rather than in a socialist direction. They express a kind of petty-bourgeois Luddite attitude towards large-scale capitalist industry. But, if Griffith had acknowledged that, in Ulster, Sinn Fein signified economic retrogression, it is unlikely that he would have attempted to resolve the contradiction at the expense of industry.

Sean Milroy (a Sinn Fein propagandist) wrote, in **The Case Of Ulster** (1922):
"the root cause of the present conditions in this corner of Ulster is nothing more nor less than an antiquated mediaeval tradition of religious ascendancy and bigotry projecting itself into the political and economic life of this section of Ireland today." (p13.)

This was an obligatory belief for the old Sinn Fein.

Nevertheless, the contradiction between nationalist aspiration and economic reality was such that it was the Sinn Fein/Republican movement which took the first steps towards creating a formal economic partition in the island. This was done in 1919/20, in the form of the "Belfast Boycott", organised by the Republican Dail. Industrial Ulster was rejecting the Sinn Fein administration which was being established everywhere else. The North was therefore to be brought to its knees through an economic boycott.

Milroy commented in 1922:
"Already the South has learned how vulnerable is the trade and commerce of the North; already, southern business has reaped advantages from the trade restrictions upon Belfast. The Southern interests that stand to benefit by a cessation of the northern trade are strong and articulate; the southern interests, if any, that stand to lose are powerless and silent… If the trade between the 6 and the 26 Counties ceases… the South will be the sole gainer and the North the sole loser. It may be well asked: why, then, in view of the solid advantages associated with separation should the South have any hankering after a political unity. The answer seems to be that the South only dimly realises the extent of these advantages, and in part that she is prepared to pay a heavy price for the maintenance of the sentimental ties of political

unity. It is, however, an open secret that the first small sample of disseverance that the South has had in the form of the boycott has, in many quarters, whetted the desire for further and more drastic action along the same lines." (ibid p96.)

The Sinn Fein historian, P.S. O'Hegarty, in **The Victory Of Sinn Fein** (1924) also dealt with the boycott. O'Hegarty says that Nationalist businessmen from Ulster, whose business suffered in the Sinn Fein/Unionist warfare, and who fled to Dublin and "forgot everything except their thirst for revenge upon Belfast", played a large part in instituting the boycott:

"The boycott started in Tuam, where the local traders and others banded together and decided to boycott all Belfast commercial travellers and goods until the expelled Nationalists should be reinstated. From Tuam the idea spread to Dublin, where the aforesaid Nationalists pushed it vigorously, and where a certain amount of unofficial boycotting began to show itself. The idea of an official boycott was raised in the Dail, and although—an astonishing fact—it was supported by Griffith, the opinion of the Dail was against it, and the division was avoided by an agreement to leave the question over for consideration and decision by the Dail Cabinet. And in the Cabinet Griffith's influence finally prevailed and the boycott was officially decreed, promulgated and enforced. It was at first nominally restricted to Belfast... but it was gradually extended, and in practice was applied to the whole of Unionist Ulster.

"The boycott itself was not the worst of the situation. It was the things which it produced that did the damage. It raised up in the south what had never been there, a hatred of the North, and a feeling that the North was as much an enemy of Ireland as was England. It made Protestant Home Rulers in the North almost ashamed of their principles, and it turned apathetic Protestant Unionists into bitter partisans. It gave the irresponsibles in the South their first taste of loot and destruction, when it used the Irish Volunteers in destroying Belfast cigarettes in small shops in Dublin, and in intercepting and destroying Belfast goods on the railways. It recognised and established real partition, spiritual and voluntary partition, before physical partition had been established and while it was still doubtful whether it would ever be established. It denied the whole principle upon which separatists of every generation had claimed for the people of this country independence. And it was absolutely ineffective. It inflicted more harm upon the Nationalists of Ulster, who had to suffer while theorists here howled hatred and boycott from a safe distance outside; it probably inflicted some damage on the Ulster majority, but it was an utter failure inasmuch it id not secure the reinstatement of a single expelled Nationalist, nor the conversion of a single Unionist. It was merely a blind suicidal contribution to the general hate." (p51-3.)

The boycott inflicted a certain amount of damage on the distributive trade in Ulster, and to a lesser extent on light industry. It made no impression whatever on the heavy industrial base of the Ulster economy.

The formal political partition of the country took place two years after the Boycott. Full account must be taken of the fact that the economic partition of Ireland was not instituted by the British, or the Unionist, governments, but by the Republican Dail elected in 1919; and that it was policed, not by British troops or B Specials, but by the IRA. While claiming national rights over Ulster, Sinn Fein and the IRA partitioned Ireland in an attempt to ruin Ulster economically, and bring it to heel.

The bureaucratic legislative illusions of the Catholic nationalist bourgeoisie are exemplified in the economic perspective outlined by Milroy in 1922. The gist of it was that the 26 Counties, having achieved national sovereignty, would outstrip Ulster economically in a brief period, and that Ulster would soon be begging to be governed by the South.

Oozing with altruism, Milroy declares that, if Ulster came in, "the south would have to sacrifice to her sentimental attachment to political unity any manufacturing ambitions which she entertains with regard to the development of the linen industry" (p86). Ulster would be allowed to retain the linen trade. But, if Ulster stayed out, a state sponsored linen industry would be developed in the South, and "it would require no gifts of prophesy to foretell at which side of the border the linen industry would be after a few years." By staying in the UK, Ulster "runs the risk, amounting to a certainty, of having the whole or greater part of her linen industry transferred to the South. There is no escape from the logic of this situation, and what is true of the linen industry is true in varying degrees of the other industries located in the North" (p86.)

This was a reasonable inference from what passed for historical fact in Nationalist propaganda. If the development of Ulster was due to accidental and external causes, or to a government favouritism towards Ulster at the expense of the South, it would have been reasonable to expect developments of the kind predicted by Milroy. If it was true that the industry of Ulster was "a growth forced by favouritism", and that "the Protestants of Ireland are at present paying the natural penalty of past monopoly, in their want of industrial efficiency" (O'Riordan: Catholicity & Progress, p263), it was reasonable to expect that there would be a collapse of industry in the North when that favouritism was ended. And, if government schemes could create thriving industries, it was reasonable to expect a flourishing of industrial development in the South. In fact, both assumptions were false. The South is no nearer to outstripping Ulster industrially today than it was fifty years ago. And, having passed through a cycle of comprehensive protectionism beginning in the early thirties (which did have the short term effect of stimulating manufactures and bringing the economic reserves of the country into play), the Southern economy wound up in the fifties in a condition of chronic stagnation, from which it escaped only by re-establishing free trade relations with Britain.

"And Pharaoh said, I will let you go; only you will not go very far away."

A Note On The First Edition

The previous editions of **The Economics Of Partition** were published in 1969, when the Irish Communist Organisation was in the process of working itself free from the Catholic nationalist conception of Irish history. While it gave a reasonably adequate account of the pure economic basis of partition, it was totally inadequate in dealing with the general social and political implications of the economic situation. While it grasped the nature of the economic basis, it failed to grasp the nature of the general social and political superstructure. The fact that it stated a more economically factual account of history than had previously been fitted into a Catholic nationalist political structure makes it a work that is treasured by 'left' Catholic nationalists today. It is a self-contradictory, transitional work combining economic sense with political nonsense. The ICO quickly superseded it, but it has been widely rehashed by various Catholic nationalist propagandists during the past couple of years.

In the first edition we wrote: "What is the 6 Counties? Nationally it is part of the Irish nation... Economically... the dominant industry has been a section of British capitalism". "The Nation" is, by implication, here conceived of as something which has nothing to do with "the economy". The economy is divided. The economic division leads to a state of war between the two economic areas. But, despite this, "the nation" remains intact. It is obvious that this concept of "the nation" had its source in the nationalist movement which had the ambition of ruling both communities: the Catholic nationalist conception of "the nation" is the area over which the Catholic bourgeoisie hopes to extend its rule.

The idea was also put forward in the first edition that the economic division within "the nation" expressed itself as a political division between the big industrial bourgeoisie of the North and the middle class of the South. Political unity could have been maintained only on the basis of the interest of the large-scale bourgeoisie. But the big bourgeoisie failed to exercise a dominant influence over "the nation" as a whole. The small capitalists and petty bourgeoisie of the South, therefore, instead of evolving under the influence of the big industrial bourgeoisie of the North, generated an independent political and economic movement of its own which came into antagonism with that of the big bourgeoisie:

> "The logic of the middle class position required the separation and protection of the Irish national market. When this bourgeois element generated a political movement of its own it came into conflict with the interests of the big industrial bourgeoisie who needed to remain in the British market. But, under the political domination of a big industrial bourgeoisie which saw the need for extensive internal reforms, the evolution of these middle class elements could have run its course without disrupting the nation." (p35.)

> "The most developed form of capitalist economy, the big industrial capitalism of the North-East, failed to develop an adequate political superstructure. The industrial capitalists, the only class on the basis of whose interests bourgeois Ireland could have been held together, failed utterly to become the dominant social and political force in the nation... As a consequence of this failure, the middle class, which in most bourgeois societies lives under the social and political hegemony of the big bourgeoisie, developed its own political and social movement and came into antagonism with the big industrial bourgeoisie. The political failure of the industrial bourgeoisie, plus the geographical concentration of big industry in the North-

East, caused the contradiction between the big and small bourgeoisie—which exists in all capitalist societies, but which is usually kept well in hand by the big bourgeoisie—to become aggravated to the point where the only solution was the political division of Ireland." (p38-9.)

Something of the same notion crops up in C.D. Greaves' book, **The Irish Crisis** (1972), and in some other quarters. Greaves, arguing against the two nations theory, writes:

"The loss of the *hinterland* across the border has been brushed aside as of negligible importance. 'The economies of the two parts of Ireland were never complementary', it is declared... The loss of the *hinterland* did not only mean the depression of the border areas, it meant the abandonment of all prospects bound up with a balanced distribution of industry." (p41.)

It is only in this particular argument (and obviously "for the sake of argument") that Greaves views the rest of the country as the economic hinterland of the North-East. Elsewhere, he treats the "hinterland" as the centre of national development.

The position stated in previous editions of The Economics Of Partition is essentially one of treating the South as the economic hinterland of the North East, which developed an economic and political life of its own due to the political inadequacy of the Northern bourgeoisie. But, while a formal case could be made for that view, it is essentially a misconception. If the South is to be conceived of as a hinterland, it should be as a hinterland of Britain.

A **Handbook Of The Ulster Question** was published by the Free State Government in 1923. It is in fact the classical statement of the one-nation position. Though it is rarely cited as a source (presumably because it was published by the Cosgraveites), and remained unknown to the B&ICO until recently, it is obvious that it has been a very influential document. The 'hinterland' argument is extensively dealt with in it. On page 106 there is a "Map showing the hinterlands served by Belfast, Derry, Enniskillen, Sligo, Newry and Dundalk in 1922 as commercial centres for the distribution of dutiable goods". The combined hinterlands of Belfast and Derry are shown as extending southwards to a line from Drogheda, through Roscommon and Tuam, to Westport. On the other hand, the Dundalk hinterland is shown as forming a triangle stretching around Enniskillen, Armagh and Banbridge. And the combined hinterlands of Sligo and Dundalk are shown as including the whole of Fermanagh.

(A map on page 104, showing the market areas served by various towns, shows substantial cross-border areas in the case of Derry, Lifford/Strabane, Enniskillen, Clones and Castleblayney.)

The purpose of the exercise is to demonstrate that "the one thing which the commercial hinterlands ignore altogether is the present artificial boundary line." (p110.) It does this to its own satisfaction by taking account of certain factors, and discreetly ignoring other very relevant factors.

Sufficient work has not yet been done on this question to deal in detail with various particular aspects of it. But what is clear is that the argument that the Border was economically artificial ignores more substantial features of the situation than it takes account of.

The wholesale distributive trade of N. Ireland undoubtedly lost part of its market as a consequence of Partition. But it would seem that the Southern border counties were on the margin where the hinterlands of Belfast and Dublin overlapped. It is also seems that the economic influence was still extending southwards at the time of Partition, and that the Northern wholesale distributive trade lost markets reaching well into the Midlands when the Customs were erected.

But the economic interest of Northern Ireland was determined by industrial, not wholesale merchant's, capital. The safeguarding of the industrial interest was of infinitely greater economic importance than the safeguarding of the outlying markets of the wholesale distributors.

Donegal seems to be an exception to the statement that the Southern border counties were in a marginal situation. It would have been more beneficial to it economically if it had been included in Northern Ireland. In this area there was certainly a conflict between national sentiment and economic interest. (But it is worth noting that the "Handbook" argues that the commercial dependence of West Donegal on Derry was politically contrived. It maintains that, when railways were being extended to West Donegal in 1890, a pressure group of Derry merchants was successful in getting the line extended from Letterkenny, round North Donegal to Burtonport—thus giving Derry access to the area—when it would have been more reasonable to extend a line upwards from South Donegal—which would have given Dublin easier access. Partition had ended Derry's monopoly of the area, and "given ordinary economic laws time to operate in a way which the merchants of Derry had long feared, and from which there is no turning back".)

But all of these matters are of secondary economic importance by comparison with the main subject of this pamphlet—the historical development of two separate economies in Ireland, and its main social and political consequence—and they will be dealt with in the detailed political history of Partition, which is in process of being published.

Though the ICO retained the idea of "the nation", as described above, it did not hold that the "national" interest "should" have taken precedence over economic development, and that the Northern economy should have been severed from the British economy for the greater glory of "the nation", even though that would have brought economic ruin to the North. But that is exactly what is held by radical Catholic nationalist organisations such as Official Sinn Fein and the Peoples' Democracy, and by a number of British Trotskyist groups.

The Khruschevite revisionists deny that there was any conflict of economic interest. Sensing that one thing leads to another, they make no concession whatsoever to historical reality. But Official Sinn Fein and the PD admit the conflict of economic interest, admit that the Northern economy required free trade with Britain for its development, and then proceed with some blatant nationalist moralising. The Northern capitalists and workers are morally condemned because they were not prepared to wreck the economy for the sake of nationalist sentiments to which they had never been attached.

This attitude is set out very well in International Socialism, April/June 1972. (IS is published by a British Trotskyist organisation which gives "unconditional support" to the Catholic bourgeois nationalist offensive to wreck the Northern economy and to subjugate the Northern Protestants). The article is written by Eamonn McCann:

> "Half a century ago the Protestants had to choose between the Union and bourgeois rule from Dublin. The protectionist economic policies of Sinn Fein, had they been applied to the North, would have bid to destroy all the Northern industrial structure. The ship-building and linen industries, cut off from sources of raw material or markets, or both, would have gone to the wall... It is not true that the Protestants, blinded by propaganda, made a crazy choice. They made a perfectly rational economic decision between the alternatives offered... This is not to argue that in 1921 the Protestants were "right" to choose to fight for the link with Britain; in so far as such monolithic

concepts [right and wrong, presumably] are applicable they were "wrong"..."
(p10).

Whatever would Trotsky, who held fifty years ago that all nationalism had ceased to serve the expansion of the productive forces and was therefore reactionary, say if he could hear these disciples of his declaring that a community was "wrong" to oppose a nationalism that would have wrecked its economy? *Why* does IS declare that the Ulster Protestant community was wrong in refusing to prostrate itself before a nationalism that would have wrecked its economy? It doesn't explain. But it can only be because the honour of the Countess Cathleen is not to be slighted out of mercenary or rational considerations.

In other circles (for example in the Socialist Workers' Movement, a group associated with B. Devlin, E. McCann and International Socialism) a very mystical concept of the "Irish nation" prevails. "The Irish nation" is attributed with what might be called 'teleological' existence. It is admitted that, in mere vulgar actuality, society in Ireland does not at present constitute, and never has constituted, a single nation. But it is destined to become a single nation. And this future destiny gives teleological national unity to present-day Ireland. What exists is not two nations, but the process-of-becoming of the metaphysically destined one nation. Elements in Official Sinn Fein and the Trotskyist International Marxist Group also adopt this position of subordinating the existent present to the non-existent future, and making the latter determine the nature of the former. Of course, every effort is made to prevent the metaphysical character of this conception from being too explicit. It has acquired any popularity only only in bourgeois intellectual circles, where the requisite obscurantist thought processes prevail.

The position of the leadership of Official Sinn Fein is made most explicit in a document entitled, **Northern Ireland And The Republican Movement**, submitted by Seamus O Tuathail (then editor of the **United Irishman**) to the Christian Student Conference in Dun Laoghaire in January 1971:

"I think I would most usefully quote the position of the main protagonists of the 'Two Nation Theory' from a policy document issued by them in Easter 1966, entitled 'The Working Class In The Irish National Revolution (1916-23)': 'Traditionally the south was nationalist and the north was Unionist. This was not due to difference in religion, in historical traditions, in racial origins or in climate. Up to the end of the 18th century the north had been the Nationalist stronghold. The reason why, in the course of the 19th century, it became the imperialist stronghold lies in the development of industrial capitalism in the North.' The above statement is... a fair analysis of why the leaders of the Northern Protestant community, all of them with imperialist connections, became amenable to the slogans of religious hatred by Carson and Smith and were so adamant in their opposition to Home Rule."

O Tuathail then proceeds with another long extract from this ICO pamphlet, which includes the following:

"Prior to 1800 it (capitalism in Ireland) needed control of the Irish market, and protection against British industry, to grow and gather strength. After 1850 the few concerns which had managed to develop into large-scale modern industries would have been ruined if they had been limited to the Irish market. Since they had not built up an Irish empire they needed access to the markets of the British Empire. This was the basis for the opposition to 'Home Rule' in the North."

O Tuathail comments: "The above quotations from an Irish Communist document of 1966 stands as an acceptable class analysis of the national struggle in Ireland and its complications down to 1900."

The "large scale modern industries" of the North East "would have been ruined if they had been limited to an Irish market." But O Tuathail does not infer from this that they should not have been forced within a protected Irish market. For your petty bourgeois nationalist the ruin of large scale industry is a small price to pay for satisfying national honour—particularly when it is the industry of another nation that is to be ruined.

Summary

The economic basis of Partition is the two distinct developments of capitalism which occurred in Ireland, at widely separated periods. The first development took place in Ulster in the latter half of the 18th century and culminated in the development of heavy industrial capitalism in the second half of the 19th century. The second took place in the South in the second half of the 19th and early 20th centuries, and fell short of the development of heavy industry.

These separate developments of capitalism in Ulster and the South at different periods did not result from the contrivances of an external force which stimulated the economic development of Ulster and repressed that of the South. It resulted from the fact that, since the early 17th century, Ireland has been inhabited by two different communities whose social structures were very different. These two communities have not been prevented from merging over the intervening three and a half centuries mainly by religious or political manipulations of a third party, but by their differing lines of economic development.

Small Commodity Production And Merchants' Capital

A Criticism (Of Sorts) A section on the above subject was omitted from the main body of this pamphlet as it seemed to be of only marginal importance. But, as we go to print, a pamphlet entitled **Ireland Upon The Dissecting Table**, by the "Cork Workers' Club" has been published (and publicised by the United Irishman), as a refutation of the previous edition of The Economics Of Partition, and also of the Two Nations theory. This refutation takes the form of a single sentence quoted from the chapter on "The Genesis Of The Industrial Capitalist" from Volume 1 of Capital, and makes it necessary to deal with the question of small commodity production in the development of the capitalist mode of production.

(A word should be said about the genesis of the Cork Workers' Club. In January 1972, under pressure of the growing Catholic nationalist offensive against the Ulster Protestant community, a couple of members of the B&ICO succumbed to Catholic nationalism, resigned from the ICO, and set up the "Cork Communist Organisation". The CCO declared that it was in general agreement with the general analysis made in **The Economics Of Partition**, **The Birth Of Ulster Unionism**, and **Connolly And Partition**, and that its sole difference with the

B&ICO was that it considered that there were two undeveloped nationalities, rather than two nations in Ireland. (This incident is dealt with in **The Irish Communist**, May and October 1971.) The CCO was soon reduced to one effective member and became defunct. He has re-emerged as the Cork Workers' Club.)

The CWC refutation of the B&ICO position is as follows:

"We have now the rather startling suggestion that from the Herculean labours of the Ulster peasantry throughout the 18th century, there came into existence (and simultaneously at that) both merchant capital and capitalist manufacture. And to top it off, it is further submitted *'this capitalism developed out of, but not on the basis of Irish society'*. One may well ask in bewilderment. 'Whither Marxism'?

"Had the genius who penned this particular line of reasoning even a passing familiarity with the rudiments of Marxism he would, perhaps, have perceived the mixture of metaphysics and Economic Materialism that form the essentials of his rationalisation. However, that aside, with respects to this business of the *natural way* of capitalist development, Marx in his 'Genesis of Industrial Capitalist' (Capital Volume 1) noted its existence, but quickly brushed it aside with the observation: *"The snail's pace of this method corresponds in no way with the commercial requirements of the new world-market that the great discoveries of the end of the 15th century created'*. The ICO in their wisdom may well scorn the capitalists 'who had not clawed their way up from the peasantry and the urban petty-bourgeoisie;' but these were the people possessing the mass of the wealth at that time, and this, on being converted into capital, laid the basis of capitalist manufacture in Ulster, as elsewhere. Marx also underscored this fact in the forementioned chapter. Of course, this is not to deny outright that some peasant weavers became small capitalists during the 18th century in Ulster. But it does reject out of hand, on the basis of Marxist theory as formulated by Marx, that a linen industry could rise in Ulster or elsewhere, which had as its fountainhead the peasant weaver. And this being so, it is ludicrous even to suggest that a middle class could evolve in Ulster, which derived an exclusive origin from the peasant-originated linen industry in the 17th and 18th centuries, and which was consequently endowed with a national identity peculiar to itself by virtue of such exclusiveness, rooted as it was in peasant origins.

"When the basis of any thesis can be shown to be spurious, it becomes unnecessary to demolish the whole, part by part. And it is well that this is generally accepted to be so, because on assessing the overall output of the ICO on Partition, the labyrinth of its perverse reasoning is simply fantastic. Indeed, an inescapable conclusion is that its greatest potential lies more in the realm of psychoanalysis than in political analysis. A psychoanalyst may well be able to deduce the mental derangement or pattern of alienation which bedevils the writer or writers" (7-8).

When the writer of the foregoing lines (which bear the inimitable style of one Jim Lane) was a member of the B&ICO, and presumably had "a passing familiarity with the rudiments of Marxism", he failed to draw attention to the self-evident absurdities of The Economics Of Partition. In fact, when other members became very dissatisfied with the previous edition of The Economics Of Partition, this belated critic of it seemed to be very happy about it, and to want to bind the B&ICO to it. And when he was leaving the B&ICO we got the impression that he considered the Economics Of Partition to be a Marxist classic, from which the B&ICO was beginning to deviate.

He never "asked in bewilderment 'Whither Marxism'?" with regard to the statement that "this capitalism developed out of Irish society, but not on the basis of Irish society". And he does not now suggest a better formulation of the matter. This formulation could undoubtedly be improved upon. But there is also no doubt that there is a peculiar relationship here which needs to be formulated. The economic relationship between Ireland and Britain since the 16th century is an exceptional phenomenon, which still awaits accurate description. At a number of points, the Irish economy (or economies, to be precise) was on the margin between being a region of the British economy and being a separate national economy. And, even when national protectionism prevailed in the South, the Southern economy still had many of the characteristics of a region of the British economy. There was sufficient economic difference to generate the aspiration of comprehensive economic separatism, but not sufficient difference to achieve it, resulting in a highly ambiguous relationship between the South and Britain. And the relationship between Ulster and Britain in the 18th century was very similar to this.

The particular formulation cited by Lane has long been felt to be unsatisfactory. In the present edition it is formulated as follows:

> "This capitalism developed out of Irish society, but not mainly on the basis of the Irish home market. The market which developed it was the British market. It was hatched out of Irish society by the British market."

Nit-picking is one thing; arriving at a more scientific formulation is another. The CWC pamphlet doesn't go beyond nit-picking.

On General Truth Which Is Independent Of The Particular Now we come to the denial that there was any essential difference in the way that capitalism was developing in Ulster, as compared with the South in the 18th century, and the assertion that merchant's capital "laid the basis of capitalist manufacture in Ulster, as elsewhere. Marx also underscored this fact in the forementioned chapter of Capital". Marx, in fact, makes no reference whatsoever to the development of capitalism in Ulster in this chapter of Capital. (And we know of nowhere that he deals with it.)

The main CWC argument is that Marx, in this chapter, established a general truth to the effect that merchant's capital (and usurer's capital should also be included) lays the basis for the development of capitalist industry wherever capitalist industry develops, and that therefore it laid the basis for its development in Ulster. This neat little piece of metaphysics enables you to know everything that is essential about the development of capitalism in Ulster, without knowing anything in particular about it. And the CWC, in fact, tells us nothing about the particular economic development of Ulster. (As it says, having dealt with the "basis", it is unnecessary to deal with "the whole, part by part".) The CWC can therefore be bracketed with those described by Lenin in The Development Of Capitalism In Russia who "endeavour to look for answers to concrete questions in the simple logical development of the general truth", and those who have not realised that "by confining oneself to general formulas... one cannot advance a single step in explaining the actual process of development of capitalism."

Marx On The Appearance Of The Capitalist In History When we turn to Capital we find that Marx is not spinning universal truths about how capitalism develops in all possible situations, and therefore in Ulster. Marx was not given to such things. What he is dealing with, in chapters on the genesis of the capitalist farmer and the industrial capitalist, is

97

the historical development of the capitalist mode of production at the end of the feudal era in Europe. He is dealing with the first historical appearance of the capitalist. He is not laying down the law about how capitalism must develop in each particular country in which a capitalist economy is developing after capitalism has become the dominant mode of production internationally. Anyone with "even a passing familiarity with the rudiments of Marxism", or even with elementary horse sense, should realise that the two are very different situations.

The relevant passages are quoted below:

"Now that we have considered the forcible creation of a class of outlawed proletarians... the question remains: whence came the capitalists originally? For the expropriation of the agricultural population creates, directly, none but great landed proprietors. As far, however, as concerns the genesis of the farmer, we can, so to say, put our hand on it, because it is a slow process evolving through many centuries. The serfs, as well as the free small proprietors, held land under very different tenures, and were therefore emancipated under very different economic conditions. In England the first form of the farmer is the bailiff, himself a serf... During the second half of the 14th century he is replaced by a farmer, whom the landlord provides with seed, cattle and implements. His condition is not very different from that of the peasant. Only he exploits more wage labour. Soon he becomes a métayer, a half-farmer. He advances one part of the agricultural stock, the landlord the other. The two divide the total product in proportions determined by contract. This form quickly disappears in England, to give place to the farmer proper, who makes his own capital breed by employing wage-labourers, and pays a part of the surplus-product, in money or kind, to the landlord as rent. So long, during the 15th century, as the independent peasant and the farm-labourer working for himself as well as for wages, enriched themselves by their own labour, the circumstances of the farmer, and his field of production, were equally mediocre. The agricultural revolution which commenced in the last third of the 15th century, and continued during the whole of the 16th... enriched him just as speedily as it impoverished the mass of the agricultural people... The continuous rise in the price of corn, wool, meat, in a word of all agricultural produce, swelled the money capital of the farmer without any action on his part, whilst the rent he paid (being calculated on the old value of money) diminished in reality. Thus they grew rich at the expense both of their labourers and their landlords. No wonder therefore, that England, at the end of the 16th century, had a class of capitalist farmers, rich, considering the circumstances of the time" (p742-4).

"The genesis of the industrial capitalist did not proceed in such a gradual way as that of the farmer. Doubtless many small guild-masters, and yet more independent small artisans, or even wage-labourers, transformed themselves into small capitalists, and (by gradually extending exploitation of wage-labour and corresponding accumulation) into full blown capitalists. In the infancy of capitalist production, things often happened as in the infancy of mediaeval towns, where the question, which of the escaped serfs should be master and which servant, was in great part decided by the earlier or later date of their flight. The snail's pace of this method corresponded in no wise with the commercial requirements of the new world-market that the great discoveries of the 15th century created. But the middle ages had handed down two distinct forms of capital, which mature in the most different economic social formations, and which, before the era of the capitalist mode of production, are considered as capital quand meme [nevertheless]—usurer's capital and merchant's capital... The money capital formed by means of usury and commerce was prevented from turning into industrial capital, in the country by the feudal constitution, in the towns by the guild organisation. These fetters vanished with the dissolution of feudal society, with the expropriation and partial eviction of the country population..." (p750-51).

"Today industrial supremacy implies commercial supremacy. In the period of manufacture properly so-called, it is, on the other hand, the commercial supremacy that gives industrial pre-dominance. Hence the predominant role of the colonial system" (p754).

The point is that the small commodity producer in the late mediaeval period did not on his own develop the capitalist mode of production. He was subject to a thousand and one feudal restrictions, to the whole conservative weight of mediaevalism. (In Europe from the 12th century onwards the small trader was the source of recurring heresies against Catholic feudalism (beginning with the Waldenses and Albigensis), and was the subject of continuous persecution, periodically taking the form of large-scale massacres, or Crusades, and culminating in the Thirty Years' War in the early 17th century). The capitalist world came into being in Holland and England through the joint action of the small producer, the merchant and the national monarchy. The merchant, at a critical moment, contributed large accumulations of traditional wealth and of wealth gained in the mercantile colonial trade. The distribution of the extensive monastic property also contributed. These large accumulations were crucial to the capitalist breakthrough. The small producer was not giving rise to capital rapidly enough to accomplish the breakthrough on his own (and he was, furthermore, strongly attached to petty bourgeois economy).

Marx On The Merchant And The Small Producer But, while the small producer did not give rise to capitalist economy, neither did merchant's or usurer's capital. Capitalist production resulted from the action of merchant's capital on an economy where there was extensive small commodity production. Marx certainly did *not* say that merchant's and usurer's capital were the basis on which capitalist production developed. He regarded merchant's capital as a catalyst, or a dissolving agent. He insisted that it could *not* develop a capitalist economy, and that the result of its activity depended not on itself but on the kind of economy on which it was acting. Merchants' capital had long existed with feudalism, without giving rise to capitalism. According to Marx:

"...merchant's capital is older than the capitalist mode of production, is, in fact, historically the oldest free state of existence of capital... Within the capitalist mode of production... merchant's capital appears merely as a capital with a *specific* function. In all previous modes of production... merchant's capital appears to perform the function *par excellence* of capital... Its existence and development to a certain level are in themselves historical premises for the development of capitalist production 1) a premise for the concentration of money wealth, and 2) because the capitalist mode of production presupposes production for trade, selling on a large scale, and not to the individual customer, hence also a merchant who does not buy to satisfy his personal wants but concentrates the purchases of many buyers in his one purchase. On the other hand, all development of merchant's capital tends to give production more and more the character of production for exchange-value, and to turn products more and more into commodities. Yet its development... is incapable by itself of promoting and explaining the transition from one mode of production to another... On the contrary, wherever merchant's capital still predominates we find backward conditions... The independent and predominant development of capital as merchant's capital is tantamount to the non-subjection of production to capital, and hence to capital developing on the basis of an alien mode of production which is also independent of it. The independent development of merchant's capital, therefore, stands in inverse proportion to the general economic development of society" (Volume 3, p320-22.)

"In the pre-capitalist stages of society commerce ruled industry. In modern society the reverse is true. Of course, commerce will have more or less of a counter-effect on the communities between which it is carried on. It will subordinate production more and more to exchange-value... Thereby it dissolves the old relationships. It multiplies money circulation. It encompasses no longer merely the surplus of production, but bites deeper and deeper into the latter, and makes entire branches of production dependant upon it. Nevertheless this disintegrating effect depends very much on the nature of the producing community. So long as merchant's capital promotes the exchange of products between undeveloped societies, commercial profit not only appears as outbargaining and cheating, but also largely originates from them... Merchant's capital, when it holds a position of dominance, stands everywhere for a system of robbery, so that its development among the trading nations of old and modern times is always directly connected with plundering, piracy, kidnapping slaves, and colonial conquest...

"Commerce, therefore, has a more or less dissolving influence everywhere on the producing organisation, which it finds to hand... What new mode of production will replace the old, does not depend on commerce, but on the character of the old mode of production itself. In the ancient world the effect of commerce and the development of merchant's capital always resulted in a slave economy... However, in the modern world, it results in the capitalist mode of production. It follows therefrom that these results spring in themselves from circumstances other than the development of merchant's capital." (p325-7.)

"The transition from the feudal mode of production is two-fold. The producer becomes merchant and capitalist, in contrast to the natural agricultural economy and the guild-bound handicrafts of the mediaeval urban industries. This is the really revolutionary path—Or else, the merchant establishes direct sway over production. However much this serves as a stepping-stone... it cannot by itself contribute to the overthrow of the old mode of production, but tends rather to preserve and retain it as its precondition... Without revolutionising the mode of production, it only worsens the condition of the direct producers, turns them into mere wage-workers and proletarians, under conditions worse than those under the immediate control of capital, and appropriates their surplus-labour on the basis of the old mode of production." (p329.)

This is a far cry from the position attributed to Marx by CWC—that merchant's capital "laid the basis of capitalist manufacture in Ulster, as elsewhere". If we are to consider either merchant's capital or the small commodity producer as the basis from which capitalist production developed, it is clear that it must be the latter. Merchants' capital is fertile in this respect only insofar as it exercises its dissolving influence on a society of small commodity producers.

Lenin On The Small Commodity Producer Lenin, too, attached particular importance to the role of the small commodity producer in the development of capitalism. (This is exemplified in his well known statement, that the small producer generates capitalism daily, hourly, and on a mass scale.):

"Despite the theories that have prevailed here during the past half-century, the Russian community peasantry are not antagonists of capitalism, but, on the contrary, are its deepest and most durable foundation. The deepest—because it is here, remote from all 'artificial' influences, and in spite of the institutions which restrict the development of capitalism, that we see the constant formation of the elements of capitalism within the 'community' itself. The most durable—because agriculture in general, and the peasantry in particular, are weighed down most heavily by the traditions of the distant past, the traditions of patriarchal life, as a consequence of which the transformative effects of capitalism... manifest themselves here most slowly and gradually." (**Development Of Capitalism**, Chapter 2, Conclusion.)

The spread of small commodity economy not only prepares society for the development of capitalism, economically and socially, and throws up capitalist manufacturers from the ranks of the independent producers, but also throws up merchant's capital from the activity of the small producers. This is not the extensive merchant's capital derived from international trade, but small scale merchant's capital, serving the development of the internal market. Lenin, in the same work, describes the development of merchant capitalists out of the ranks of the small producers in Russia. In particular, he describes their development from the independent producers in the lace industry in Moscow.

"The 'tradeswomen' came into being in the following way. In the 1820s... when the number of lace makers was still small, the principal buyers were the landlords, the 'gentry'. The consumer was in the neighbourhood of the producer. As the industry spread, the peasants began to send their lace to Moscow 'as the chance offered', for example, through comb-makers. The inconvenience of this primitive marketing very soon made itself felt. The sale of lace was entrusted to one of the lace-makers, who was compensated for the time she lost. 'She also brought back thread for the lace' [these are quotes from a Government Report quoted by Lenin]. Thus the inconvenience of isolated marketing led to turning trade into a special function performed by one person who gathered the wares from the lace-makers. Production for sale teaches that time is money. It becomes necessary to compensate the intermediary for her lost time and labour; she becomes accustomed to this occupation and begins to make it her profession. 'Journeys of this kind, repeated several times, gave rise to the *tradeswoman type*'. The woman who has been to Moscow several times establishes the permanent connections which are so necessary for proper marketing... 'The tradeswomen begin... to bring goods from the towns and make a considerable profit.' The commission agent thus becomes an independent trader who now begins to monopolise sales and to take advantage of her monopoly to subjugate the lace-makers completely. Usurious operations appear alongside commercial operations—the lending of money to the lace-makers, the taking of goods from them at reduced prices, etc.... To which it should be added that such types develop from among the small producers themselves. 'However many enquiries we made, we found that all the tradeswomen had formerly been lace-makers themselves, and consequently, were familiar with the trade;... they had no capital to start with, and had only gradually begun to trade in callico and other goods, as they made money out of their commissions.' There can be no doubt, therefore, that under commodity economy, not only prosperous industrialists in general, but also, and particularly, representatives of merchant's capital emerge from among the small producers." (Chapter 5, Section 6.)

(To which it should be added that most of the great merchant and banking families of the modern world developed from such small commodity origins, rather than from the mediaeval merchant families.)

The Matter Of Fact The CWC's universal truth of Marxism turns out to be a metaphysical fabrication which is all its own work. The B&ICO has concerned itself with attempting to discover how in actual fact capitalism developed in Ireland. It did not adopt the magician's approach of the CWC, which tries to spin knowledge of a particular situation out of generalisations about the development of capitalism in general. And, rather than checking at every moment that we were saying nothing that was heretical with relation to Capital, we took it for granted that if we succeeded in describing how capitalism actually developed in Ireland we would not come into contradiction with Marx's general analysis of capitalism. And so it transpires.

Which leaves only the question of whether we have, in its main outlines, accurately described the particular way in which capitalism developed in Ireland. But, about the particular, the CWC has nothing to say. Its position is the simple metaphysical one that merchant's capital lays the basis for capitalist manufacture everywhere, therefore in Ulster and in Southern Ireland. Now there was plenty of merchant's capital in the South in the later 18th century—more than in the North. But the South in this period displays essentially the characteristics of the action of merchant's capital on a semi-feudal economy, whereas Ulster displays the signs of a society where matters are proceeding by the "revolutionary path", whereby "the producer becomes merchant and capitalist". This is not to deny that there was the intervention of merchant's capital in Ulster; it is to say that the nature of the effect of merchant's capital in Ulster was determined by the fact that capitalist industry was being generated by a strong economy of small commodity producers.

A number of peculiarities of Ulster Protestant society relevant to this issue should be noted here. The Ulster Plantation, like the American Plantation of the same period, took place at the beginning of the bourgeois era, and was made up for the most part of the more adventurous spirits from the small producers of one of the first bourgeois nations, who were still subject to hangovers of feudal restriction and oppression at home. The new Ulster Plantation society developed without feudal institutions. On the land, a class of tenant-farmers prevented the growth of absolute landowners. The towns were more or less free from the restrictive practices of the guild. The law was bourgeois law. And the society lay close to the greatest capitalist market of the period. And, in its various phases of development, it bears the hallmark of an industrial society which has evolved from a small commodity basis, rather than a society to which merchant's capital has given its atmosphere.

Belfast And The Slave Trade Belfast's contribution to the slave trade, (to which merchant's capital was attracted like flies to a honey pot), shows how much the spirit of the merchant capitalist prevailed there. In 1786 it dawned on a number of Belfast bourgeoisie that they were neglecting an opportunity to capture some of the great profits that were to be made in the slave trade. A meeting of men of business was called to organise an enterprise in that activity, and to found a Belfast Slave-Ship Company. Midway through a discussion of the business side of the enterprise, the view was expressed that trade in men was wicked and unchristian. There was general agreement that it was. And that was the beginning and the end of the slave trade of Belfast.

> "Thomas M'Cabe was a watchmaker in North Street. He erected the first cotton mill in Ireland, with Henry Joy and Capt. J. M'Cracken as partners. When asked to sign a contract with other Belfast merchants for embarking in the slave trade, he used these remarkable words—"May God wither the hand and consign the name to eternal infamy of the man who will sign that document.' The scheme therefore fell through." (**Historical Notes Of Old Belfast**, p269.)

Nationality And The International Market   The point of this piece of CWC mystification is to refute the Two Nations theory. The CWC apparently considers that the nationality of the Ulster Protestant community is dependent on there being an Ulster middle class "which derived an exclusive origin from a peasant-originated linen industry of the 17th and 18th centuries, and which was consequently endowed with a national identity, peculiar to itself by virtue of such an exclusiveness". It gives no reason whatever for this assumption. And it need only be said that if the fact that the Ulster capitalist class did not develop exclusively out of the small producers refutes the claim of the Ulster Protestant community to national rights, it is an even stronger point against the claims of the Catholic community to national rights. But this idea of exclusiveness has nothing to do with the real world. Marx pointed out

> "the villainies of the Venetian thieving system formed one of the secret bases of the capital-wealth of Holland to whom Venice in her decadence lent large sums of money. So also was it with Holland and England. By the beginning of the 18th century the Dutch manufacturers were far outstripped. Holland had ceased to be the nation preponderant in commerce and industry. One of its main lines of business, therefore, from 1701-1776, is the lending of enormous amounts of capital, especially to its great rival England. The same thing is going on today between England and the United States. A great deal of capital, which appears to-day in the United States without any certificate of birth was yesterday in England." (Volume 1, p755-6.)

The method by which the CWC negates Ulster Protestant nationality, would lead here to the negation of Dutch, English and American nationality. But: "The world market forms the basis for this mode of production." (Marx.)

National capitalist development, therefore, takes place within the world market, and not in totally isolated national economic units. And the movement of capitalists from country to country is a constant feature in the world market. Ireland has always had a particularly intimate relationship with the British market, which the most extreme developments of separatist nationalism did not seriously interfere with. But the interconnection with Britain, and the nationalism, are *both* historical realities. To assert that the Ulster Protestant community is not entitled to national rights, unless it can be shown that capital accumulation in Ulster came exclusively from the native small producers has nothing in common with the Marxist approach—and, if consistently applied, would lead not merely to the denial of Ulster Protestant nationality, but of all nationality in Ireland.

Ireland may be conceived of economically as two distinct and dissimilar regions of the British economy, with less injustice to historical fact than is involved in the conception of Ulster and the South as two regions of a common national economy.

Bibliography

Belfast Chamber Of Commerce	Report Of Meeting With Gladstone In 1893
Biggar, F.J.	The Ulster Land War Of 1770 (1910)
Campbell, G.	The Irish Land (1869)
Chart, D.A.	Economic History Of Ireland (1920)
Coe, W.E.	The Engineering Industry In The North Of Ireland (1969)
Communist Party Of Northern Ireland	Ireland's Path To Socialism (1963)
Connolly, J.	Labour In Irish History (1910)
Crommelin, Louis	An Essay Towards The Improving Of The Hempen And Flaxen Manufacture In Ireland (1703
Crotty, R.	Irish Agricultural Production (1966)
Cullen, L.M.	An Economic History Of Ireland Since 1660 (1972)
" " (edit.)	The Formation Of The Irish Economy (1969)
D'Alton, E.A.	History Of Ireland (1903)
Davis, T.	Thinker & Teacher (Selection by Arthur Griffith)
Devon Commission On Land Occupation In Ireland	Report of (1845)
Duffy, C.G.	The League Of North & South (1886)
Gill, C.	The Rise Of The Irish Linen Industry (1925)
Greaves, C.D.	Wolfe Tone And The Irish Nation (1963)
" "	The Irish Crisis (1972)
Hancock, W. Neilson	The Tenant Right Of Ulster Considered Economically (1845)
Her Majesty's Stationery Office (Belfast)	Irish Economic Documents (1867)
Irish Workers' Party	Ireland Her Own (1963)
Kane, R.R.	Industrial Resources Of Ireland (1844)
Lalor, F.	Tenant Law And Landlord Law (1847)
" "	To The Landowners Of Ireland (1847)
Lecky, W.E.H.	Democracy And Liberty (1899)
Lenin	The Development Of Capitalism In Russia
Leyburn, J.G.	The Scotch-Irish (1962)
MacDonald, Walter	Some Ethical Questions Of Peace And War (1919)
" "	Postscript (to above) (1920)
M'Knight, J.	The Ulster Tenant-Right (1848)
Marx	Capital (Volumes 1 & 3)
Milroy, Sean	The Case Of Ulster (1922)
Montgomery, W.E.	History Of Land Tenure In Ireland (1899)
Murray, A.E.	Commercial Relations Between England And Ireland (1603)
"Nationality"	(Sinn Fein Newspaper, Ed. A. Griffith, 1918 and 1919)
North Eastern Boundary Bureau (Stationery Office, Dublin)	A Handbook Of The Ulster Question (1923)
O'Brien, George	Economic History Of Ireland In The 17th Century (1919)
" "	Ibid, in the 18th Century (1918)
" "	Introduction to "Modern Irish Trade" by E.J. O'Riordan (1920)
" "	The Economic Effects Of The Reformation (1923)
" "	The Phantom Of Plenty (1948)
Petty, W.	Political Anatomy Of Ireland (1691)
Plunkett, H.	Ireland In The New Century (1905)
Public Record Offic (Northern Ireland)	Aspects Of Irish Social History (1969)
Sigerson, G.	History Of Land Tenure And Land Classes In Ireland ((1870)
Stephenson, R.	Inquiry Into The State And Progress Of Linen Manufacture (1757)
Solow, B.L.	The Land Question And The Irish Economy, 1870-1903 (1970)
Woodburn, J.B.	The Ulster Scot (1914)
Young, A.	Tour In Ireland (1776)
Young, R.M.	Historical Notices Of Old Belfast (1896)

Index

Albigenses 99
Antrim (Co.) 42, 44
Armagh (Co.) 41, 42
Ascendancy 16, 35 79

Ballycalcatt 25
Ballykinney 25
Ballymena 86
Ballywalter 25
Banbridge 42, 86
B&ICO 10, 17, 53, 60, 95-6, 102
Bank of Ireland 45
Bann, River 27
BBC 17
Belfast 42-45, 54, 82, 84-6, 92, 102
"Belfast Boycott" 88-9
Bew, P. 58
B-Specials 89
Biggar, F.J. 25
Brehon Laws 19
Brown, Daniel Gun 27
Butt, Isaac 78

Calvin, J. 68
Cambric 4
Campbell, G. 32-33
Capital 96-8
Carson, E. 94
Castlereagh, Lord 29
Chant, D.A. 13, 37
Chichester, Arthur 19, 60
China 80
Civil Rights movement 17
Clark, Dr. (Rector of Armagh) 26
Clarke, George 85
Clifford, A. 72
Coates, Victor 83
Cobbett, W. 59
Cobden 13
Coe, W.E. 82
Compradores 15
Connolly, J. 12-4, 51, 53, 77, 79
Communist Party Of Great Britain 12
Communist Party Of Ireland 15
Communist Party of Northern Ireland 15-17
Connolly Association 12
Coogan, T.P. 49
Cooke, H. 62
Coombe, James 83
Cork (City) 55, 82
Cork Communist Orgn. 95
Cork Workers' Club 95-7, 102
Corn 51-2
Cornwallis, Lord 29

Cotten, Stephen 82
Cotton 43, 46
Crawford, Wm. Sharman 56
Crommelin, Louis 38
Crotty, R. 51, 70-71, 73, 76, 78
Cullen, L.M. 48, 51, 53, 58-9, 81-2

Dáil Eireann 88-9
D'Alton, Rev. E.A. 25
Damask 41
Davies, Sir John 18-19
Davis, Thomas 28
Davitt, M. 60
Defenders 44
Derry 14, 45, 92-3
Devlin, Bernadette 24
Devon Commission 22-4, 27-8, 48
Donegal (County) 93
Donegall, Lord 25-6
Down (Co.) 41-4
Drogheda 42, 92
Dromore 43
Dublin 12, 14, 45, 72, 82
Duffy, Charles G. 21-1, 34
Drumlee, Co. Down 27
Drummond, Thomas 32
Dundalk 38
Dun Laoghaire 94

Edenderry 25
Engels, F. 72, 78
Enniskillen 92

Famine 34, 72-6
Farrell, M. 17, 54
Fianna Fáil 79
Fine Gael 79
Fintan Lalor (see Lalor, F.)
Foster 51
Fox, G. 59
France 38

Gaelic Athletic Assoc. (GAA) 80
Gaelic League 80
Gilford 26
Gill, C. 12-4, 38, 40, 42-3, 45, 51
Gladstone, W.E. 54, 84, 86
Grattan's Parliament 13, 29, 48-54, 63
Gray, J. 17
Greaves, C.D. 12-3, 16-8, 20, 24, 53, 92
Green Boys (see Oakboys)
Greg, John 25
Griffith, A. 15, 28, 45, 88
Guardian, The 17

105

Haarlem 41
Hancock, J. 22, 27, 30
Harland, E.J.H. 83, 85
Healy, T.P. 79
Hill, G. 25
Hillsborough 43
Hind, John 82
Holland 41, 99, 103
Home Rule 12, 15, 45, 84, 94
Honer, George 82-3
HMSO, Belfast 29
Huxley, T. 68
Huguenots 37-8, 40, 57

ICO 91, 93-4, 96
IMG 94
Internationalists 9
International Socialism (Group) 17, 94
International Socialism (Magazine) 17, 72, 93
IRA 89
Irish Democrat 53
Irish Workers' Party 15-17
Italy 80

Jamaica 55
Jansenism 76
Johnston, Mr. 26
Joy, Henry 46, 103

Kane, R.R. 37, 65-6, 83
Kautsky, K. 9
Kerry (Co.) 59
Knox, J. 68

Labour Party, British 11
Lalor, F. 73-5
Land League 31, 56, 60
Lavoleye 35
Lecky 25, 35
Legoniel 25
Lenin 14, 36, 39, 41-2, 50, 59, 60, 90, 97, 101
Leyburn, J.G. 22
Limerick 57
Linen 46
Linen Hall Library 17
Lisburn 38, 42, 86
Londonderry (City) 86
Londonderry (County) 42, 44
Londonderry, Lord 29
Lurgan 26, 86
Lurgan, Lord 22, 27
Luther, M. 68

McCabe 46
McCann, Éamonn 17, 93

McCracken 46, 103
MacDonald, Rev. W. 54-5
M'Knight, James 21, 31
MacNeill, Eoin 40
Mayo, Co. 59

Mackie, James 83
Mangan, James Clarence 76
Marx, K. 11, 22, 28, 31-2, 50, 53, 58, 61, 69, 72, 78, 80, 96, 99-100, 103
Marxism Today 12
Milroy, Seán 88, 90
Monaghan (Co.) 44
Montgomery, W.E. 21, 30, 34
Moore, G.H. 78
Mulholland, John 44
Murray, A. 62
Murray, A.E. 47

Newtownards 29
Newtownhamilton 27
Northern Star (PD) 17, 54

O'Brien, George 13, 46-8, 52-3, 58, 60, 62-3, 69-70, 88
O'Connell, D. 12, 62, 78
O'Doherty, Sir Cahir 21
O'Donnell, P. 11-12
O'Hegarty, P.S. 89
O'Neill's Rebellion 18-19
O'Riordain, Rev. M. 50, 63, 68-9, 90
O Tuathail, Séanys 94-5

Oakboys 25
Official Sinn Féin 93-4
Orange Order 9, 44, 81

Palmer, J. 17
Parliament (Irish) 45-6, 50, 52-3
Parnell 79
Penal Laws 15-6, 19-20
People's Democracy 17, 54, 93
Petty, William 47
Plantation 18, 20
Planters 16
Plunkett, Horace 67-8
Porter, James 27
Port Stewart 27
Powell, Mr. 27
Presbyterians 20, 22, 24, 31
PRONI 26, 28

Quakers 59

Radio Ulster 17
Redmond, J. 79
Repeal 53

106

Ricardo, D. 32, 69
Rider, Job 82
Ruhr 15

Scotland 20, 22-4, 31
Sharman Crawford, W. (see Crawford, W. Sharman)
Sigerson, G. 19-20
Sinclair, Thomas 84
Sinn Féin 45, 50, 5-5, 58, 79, 8-9
Smith, F.E. 94
Socialist Party Of Ireland 11
Socialist Workers' Party (see IS) 17, 94
Solow. B.L. 56-8
Spain 80
Spencer, P. 46
Stainton, Edward 83
Stafford, Earl of (see Wentworth, T.)
Stephenson 13, 38-9
Stewart (Londonderry, Ld.) 29
Stopford Green, Alice 46

The Times **(London) 31**
Tipperary 32
Tobacco 55
Tone, Wolfe 18
Trotskyists 54, 60
Tuam 84

Tyrone 42, 44

Ulster 9, 12, 14, 16, 17-23, 25, 28, 33, 37, 39, 41-45, 50, 57, 71-4, 78, 81, 87, 90, 95-7, 102
Ulster Custom 14-6, 18-21, 23-4, 27, 33, 34-5, 50, 56-8
Ulster Unionist 62
Unionism 9-10, 84, 88
Unionist 52, 54
United Irishmen 29, 46, 52-3
United Kingdom 85

Vatican 80
Volunteer Movement 16, 46, 54

Waldenses 99
Wentworth, Thomas 37, 46
Wexford 29, 82
Whigs 78
Wolfe Tone (See Tone, Wolfe)
Woodburn, J.B. 22
Wool 46-7, 50
Woolf, H. 83

Young, Arthur 26, 57, 76
Young Ireland 21
York Street, Belfast 44

ATHOL BOOKS DISTRIBUTION SERVICE

"The Labour Opposition" Of Northern Ireland, Introduced by Joe Keenan. Reprint of entire run of this Belfast paper of 1925/6, Athol Books, 1992, ISBN 0 85034 054 3

The Origin Of Irish Catholic-Nationalism. Selections from Walter Cox's "Irish Magazine": 1807-1815, Introduced and Edited by Brendan Clifford, Athol Books, ISBN 0 85034 53 5

Ireland In The Great War (The Irish Insurrection of 1916 Set In Its Context Of The World War by Charles James O'Donnell (1849-1934) and Brendan Clifford), Athol Books, ISBN 0 85034 055 1

Irish Education: The Case For Secular Reform by David Alvey
Preface by Michael D. Higgins, TD. Experiences of the system, the facts and figures, historical appendices. Church & State Books and Athol Books, 1991, ISBN 0 85034 047 0

Faith And Fatherland by Fr. Pat Buckley
The Irish News, The Catholic Hierarchy And The Management Of Dissidents
Belfast Historical &Educational Society, 1991, ISBN 1 872078 02 8

The Veto Controversy by Brendan Clifford
Including Thomas Moore's Letter To The Roman Catholics Of Dublin (1810).
Athol Books, 1985, ISBN 0 85034 030 6

Scripture Politics by Rev. William Steel Dickson, *The Most Influential United Irishman Of The North. Introduced and edited by Brendan Clifford.*
Athol Books, 1991, ISBN 0 85034 044 6

Billy Bluff And The Squire (A Satire On Irish Aristocracy) by Rev. James Porter, *who was hanged in the course of the United Irish Rebellion of 1798.* Introduced and edited by Brendan Clifford. Athol Books, 1991, ISBN 0 85034 045 4

The Causes Of The Rebellion In Ireland by Rev. Thomas Ledlie Birch, *who was exiled after being courtmartialed during the rebellion of 1798.* Introduced and edited by Brendan Clifford. Athol Books, 1991, ISBN 085034 046 2

Belfast In The French Revolution by Brendan Clifford
Extracts from the United Irish paper, the Northern Star. Belfast Historical & Educational Society, 1989, ISBN 1 872078 00 1

Thomas Russell And Belfast by Brendan Clifford. *Account of 18th Belfast and of "The Man From God Knows Where". Extracts from Russell's Journal, and his satire, Lion Of Old England,* Athol Books, 1988, ISBN 085034 033 0

Derry And The Boyne by Nicholas Plunket. *A Contemporary Account of The Siege Of Derry, The Battle Of The Boyne and The General Condition Of Ireland In the Jacobite War.* Introduced by Brendan Clifford. Belf. Hist. & Educ. Soc. ISBN 1 872078 01 X

The O'Neill Years by David Gordon
Unionist Politics 1963-1969. Athol Books, 1989, ISBN 085034 039 X

From Civil Rights To National War by Pat Walsh
Northern Ireland Catholics Politics 1964-74. Athol Books, 1989, ISBN 085034 040 3

Northern Ireland And The Algerian Analogy: A Suitable Case For Gaullism? by Hugh Roberts. Critique of colon theory. Athol Books, 1986, ISBN 085034 031 4

The Constitutional History Of Eire/Ireland by Angela Clifford
Post-1921 Constitutional developments, set in their political context. Athol Books, 1987, ISBN 085034 032 2

The Life And Poems Of Thomas Moore by Brendan Clifford
Athol Books, 1984, ISBN 085034 029 9

The Dubliner: The Lives, Times And Writings Of James Clarence Magan by Brendan Clifford. Athol Books, 1988, ISBN 085034 036 5

A Story Of The Armada by Captain Francisco De Cuellar, Joe Keenan and others. *Additional material by Madawc Williams, Pope Sixtus the Fifth and Admiral Monson.* Athol Books (for Bel. Hist. & Educ. Soc.), 1988, ISBN 085034 037 3

Poor Law In Ireland by Angela Clifford. *Historical review starting in 1838, detailed account of 1932 Outdoor Relief Dispute, refutation of Paddy Devlin's book on subject.* Athol Books, 1983, ISBN 085034 033 0 (a 163-page, A4 pamphlet)

All the books are available postfree, by mail order only, from:

Athol Books,
10 Athol Street, Belfast, BT12 4GX
SEND FOR A FULL CATALOGUE